**PEARSON**  ALWAYS LEARNING

# Academic Writing Essentials

Second Edition

**Department of English**
**University of Victoria**
**2011**

Pearson Learning Solutions, 501 Boylston Street, Suite 900, Boston, MA 02116
A Pearson Education Company
www.pearsoned.com

Printed in Canada

   13 XXXX 16 15 14


000200010270788189

MHB

ISBN 10: 1-256-35079-6
ISBN 13: 978-1-256-35079-8

# ACKNOWLEDGEMENTS

For their help with the second edition, we are grateful to the following members of the Department of English: Monika Rydygier Smith, Joe Gibson, Janelle Jenstad, Suzan Last, Erin Kelly, Brian Day, Heidi Darroch, Eric Henderson, Lynnette Kissoon, and Bernard LaVie.

The first edition of *Academic Writing Essentials* was prepared by the following faculty and recent graduates from the University of Victoria's Department of English and staff and tutors from the Writing Centre.

## Contributors: Department of English

- Susan Doyle, Writing Program Adviser, Department of English
- Jenny Duggan, BA (English), Professional Writing Minor
- Julia Fabian, BA (Writing), Professional Writing Minor
- Rachel Dunn, BA (English), Professional Writing Minor

We thank the following members of the English department for their ideas, comments, and support: Kim Blank, Elizabeth Grove-White, Eric Henderson, Janelle Jenstad, Arnie Keller, Erin Kelly, Bernard LaVie, Robert Miles, Leina Pauls, Richard Pickard, Harb Sanghara, Monika Rydygier Smith, Lisa Surridge, Tara Thomson, Adrienne Boyarin Williams.

We are especially grateful to Jenny Duggan for her contributions to the writing, editing, copyediting, and proofreading of the guide and to Rare Software and Communications, Ltd., for generously contributing the design and layout of the guide.

*Academic Writing Essentials* was inspired by and incorporates portions of the *University of Victoria Writer's Guide*, which was published in several editions between 1991 and 2008. We acknowledge and thank the authors, Paul MacRae, Kim Blank, and Michael Best.

## Contributors: The Writing Centre

- Laurie Waye, Coordinator, The Writing Centre
- Michael Lukas, Tutor, PhD student in English
- Carolyn Pytlyk, Tutor, PhD candidate in Linguistics
- Sean Chester, Tutor, PhD student in Computer Science
- Liam Mitchell, Tutor, PhD candidate in Cultural Studies and Political Thought
- Karen Sloan, Tutor, PhD candidate in Law
- Brenda Proctor, Tutor, MA (English)
- Shu-Min Huang, Tutor, MA (Linguistics)

We thank the following people for their contributions to the guide: Teresa Dawson and Marg MacQuarrie, Learning & Teaching Centre, and Inba Kehoe, Mearns Centre for Learning.

Susan Doyle
Laurie Waye
Editors, *Academic Writing Essentials*

# PART I: ACADEMIC WRITING

# Introduction to Academic Writing

Good academic writing skills are essential to your success as a student. They will enable you to learn more effectively, to pursue your academic interests more deeply, and to earn better grades. They will also prepare you for the professional world, where the same advanced writing skills you will use as a student are highly valued.

As a university student, you are entering a well-established academic community, which, like all communities, has its own ways of using language and its preferred ways of communicating. Understanding what they are is the first step in becoming a good academic writer.

## CHARACTERISTICS OF ACADEMIC WRITING

Whatever your previous experiences as a writer, as a university student, you will be using language in ways that might be new to you. Here are some of the characteristics of academic writing that distinguish it from other ways of writing and using language.

**It builds on the ideas and research of others.** Building knowledge is the work of the academic community. As a student, the knowledge you are building is your own. When you write at university, you study the ideas and research of others and then demonstrate your knowledge in your own words, building on the ideas you have read and crediting the people whose ideas you have used.

**It uses a specific kind of evidence.** Academic writing is based primarily on evidence, rather than on opinion, belief, or personal experience. An incident that happened to a friend or an example that is not documented in other people's writing is usually not considered acceptable evidence. Likewise, most popular media, such as magazines, TV shows, and websites, are not considered reliable sources in academic writing.

**It makes a point.** Academic writing usually begins with a thesis statement in the first paragraph. The thesis states the point you are making. The rest of the paper provides your reasoning and evidence to support your point. The conclusion reminds the reader of what you have told them, and why it is important. This pattern is echoed at the paragraph level: the thesis statement is called a topic sentence, and opens the paragraph. It is followed by sentences that support that statement.

**It uses formal language.** Academic writing uses serious, formal language. It rarely uses a sensational, passionate, or emotional tone, or casual language. For example, most disciplines discourage the use of the first person (statements such as "I think that the statistics are persuasive"). Academic writing usually avoids slang and the use of contractions. You can learn the preferred writing style of your discipline by reading textbooks and journal articles in that discipline. You can learn the preferred style of your instructor by asking for guidance about what is acceptable and what is not.

**It is different in different disciplines.** Some aspects of academic writing are the same in all disciplines, but many disciplines have their own preferences. The writing you do in an English course will be different from the writing you do in a biology course. The best way to find out what kind of writing is expected in your discipline is to look at the readings you are assigned. Do you see the word "I" or does the author avoid using it?

How is the text organized? Another way to find out is to ask your instructors how they expect you to write.

**It is different in different cultures.** If you were educated in a different culture or in a different language, it is important for you to know that the academic writing done at a North American university may be different from what you are used to. For example, in some cultures, it is considered condescending to state your ideas explicitly. However, in North American academic writing, writers are expected to state their ideas directly and clearly. The way the ideas of others are cited may also be different from what you are used to. If you are writing a paper for readers from your own culture, then what is common knowledge, and therefore does not need to be cited, is different. If you are in doubt, always check with your instructor.

## BECOMING A BETTER ACADEMIC WRITER

Regardless of how experienced a writer you are or how well you write now, your academic writing will naturally improve the more you write. With every paper you plan, research, draft, and edit, you will not only gain academic knowledge but also hone your academic writing skills. Here are some other ways you can work on becoming a better academic writer.

**Assess yourself.** Inside the cover of this guide is a chart you can use to assess your level of competence in ten key academic writing skills. Use the questions to identify skills that you need to work on, to develop a plan to strengthen your skills in those areas, and to check your progress periodically. Becoming more aware of what you do as an academic reader and writer is a good starting point for improving your skills.

**Use this guide and its companion resources.** Once you have assessed your skills, check the table of contents of this guide to see which sections address the skills you want to improve. In addition, your purchase of *Academic Writing Essentials* gives you a year's access to MyCanadianCompLab, a collection of easy-to-use and useful online resources, including tutorials, writing samples, and exercises. MyCanadianCompLab includes a complete online writing environment, with documentation style guides, dictionaries, a link to EBSCOhost and six free online tutoring sessions. Take a minute to register your subscription, then explore and use the resources.

**Examine academic writing.** One of the best ways to learn how to write academically is to look closely at textbooks and journal articles in your discipline. You will find examples of how to incorporate quotations in a paper and how to format the references section. You can even look at how different authors write their introductions and conclusions in order to get new ideas. If the writing in the textbook or article is clear and concise, then use it as a model for your own writing.

**Get help with your writing.** If you are struggling with your writing, check to see what resources are available on campus and set aside time to make use of them. If you need help with your academic assignments, visit the Writing Centre, or talk to your instructor or your TA (teaching assistant). If you are having time management problems, visit the Learning Skills Centre. If you are having problems dealing with stress, visit Counselling Services.

## Understanding Your Instructors' Comments

Another way to become a stronger academic writer is to use the comments you receive on your academic writing assignments to identify what you need to work on.

Here are some common comments instructors use when grading a writing assignment and what they mean.

**"Wordy" or "Awkward" or "Be concise"** Wordiness means using more words than are necessary to express your idea. When you look through your draft, highlight sentences that are long. Focus on one sentence at a time. Do you need all the words you've used, or is there a better, shorter way to write the sentence? Here is an example of a sentence that uses too many words, followed by a clearer, more concise version.

| | |
|---|---|
| Original | The enforcement of the second-language requirements for students at the college has not been successful for the reason that it is difficult to establish standard guidelines surrounding universal evaluations of grades from a number of various colleges and universities. |
| Improved | The college has not successfully enforced second-language requirements because it has not yet established standard evaluation guidelines. |

**"Unclear" or "Be clear" or "?"** Comments like these mean your sentence is either vague—the information is not specific enough—or confusing to the reader, often because it contains too much information. Here is an example of an unclear statement, followed by a clearer version that allows the reader to understand the author's meaning.

| | |
|---|---|
| Original | Although not a primary focus, the differences between speech types—conversation and passage—were taken into consideration in the analysis in the present study. The following charts provide the visual for the differences and/or relationship between the two speech types in the production of the participants in the four dialects we examined. |
| Improved | The present study examined the differences between speech types—conversation and passage. The results from the analysis are outlined in the following charts. |

**"Support your claim" or "What's your evidence?"** Comments like these tell you that you have not provided evidence from other, published works. This often happens when you use a generalization. Instead, find evidence to support your statement.

| | |
|---|---|
| Original | Chinese people are good at music. |
| Improved | Native speakers of tonal languages have been found to be almost nine times more likely to possess perfect pitch (Deutsch, 2004). |

**"What's your source? or "Cite sources"** Comments like these are similar to the previous comments, but there is one main difference. In the previous situation, the instructor has asked you to provide evidence. In this situation, the instructor has asked you to document your source—that is, to state where you found the information. You may have included a paraphrase or a quotation but forgotten to include the citation, or you may have included a statistic without noting which journal article it came from.

| | |
|---|---|
| Original | The Myers-Briggs Type Indicator is based on the typological theories and includes four dichotomies. |
| Improved | The Myers-Briggs Type Indicator (Briggs & Myers, 1962) draws from Carl Jung's typological theories (1921/1923) and includes four dichotomies. |

**"Pay attention to grammar" or "Proofread your paper"** Comments like these are self-explanatory. Your instructor is telling you to reread your work to ensure that you have caught all the little mistakes that can affect the reader's enjoyment or under-standing of your paper, and therefore your grade. When you are satisfied that the ideas expressed in your assignment are clear and the paragraphs are well organized, be sure to spend some time checking that each sentence is correct and that your work is free of spelling, grammar, punctuation, capitalization, and other errors.

| | |
|---|---|
| Original | The recent snowstorm on Vancouver <u>island</u> caused <u>wide-spread damage to many</u> farms on the <u>Sanich</u> Peninsul<u>a, a</u> major part of the damage <u>occured</u> to local greenhouses <u>that failed to stand up under the weight of the snow that accumu-lated on top of them.</u> |
| Improved | The recent snowstorm on Vancouver <u>Island</u> caused <u>wide-spread damage to farms</u> on the <u>Saanich</u> Peninsul<u>a. Much </u>of the damage was sustained by local greenhouses that <u>col-lapsed under the weight of the accumulated snow.</u> |

# The Academic Writing Process: 40/20/40

Like many students, you may sometimes find yourself struggling with your academic writing assignments. For example, you may have experienced one or more of the following problems:

- You put off your writing until the last moment, then dash off a draft the night before an assignment is due. Even though you end up with a passing grade, you don't feel you really understood what you wrote, and you certainly didn't find the writing easy.

- You spend so much time researching and writing your first draft that you run out of time before you can edit, revise, or proofread. The paper you submit contains both minor errors, in grammar and punctuation, and major errors, in the organization and structure of your essay.

- You want to make every sentence perfect before you have a complete draft, and end up with a paper with a strong beginning and a rushed, error-filled ending.

Besides the obvious problems with these approaches, they will leave you feeling stressed and flustered, and result in lower grades than you would like.

The process that works best for many students has three stages, of which writing is actually the shortest. The academic writing process can be demonstrated by the ratio 40/20/40: the first forty percent of your time is spent planning, the middle twenty percent is spent writing, and the last forty percent is spent revising and editing.

By structuring your time according to this ratio, you will write more efficiently because you can focus on one stage at a time rather than weaving the three stages together, rushing your work, or feeling overwhelmed by the work you have to do.

## THE FIRST 40: PLANNING YOUR WRITING

The planning stage includes developing a topic, researching, making notes, organizing your information, and structuring your argument. A good way to get started with planning a paper is by reading lightly and developing a topic. You then begin to research that topic in depth, guided by specific research questions. For advice on how to do this effectively, review "Choosing and Narrowing Your Topic" on page 84 and "Tips for Choosing a Research Topic" on page 30.

### The Zero Draft

While you are reading and researching, you should keep track of your thoughts and work for later use. It is a good idea to gather your ideas in one document, sometimes called the **zero draft**, before you begin writing your first draft.

To create a zero draft, gather all the information you might want to use and organize it based upon your ideas and initial arguments.

Here are some things you might want to include in your zero draft:

- your intial ideas and arguments
- facts, figures, and data
- quotations and where you found them
- a rough outline of your paper
- free-writing, journaling, and mind mapping

## Why Not Just Start Writing?

It's hard to create a good first draft if you aren't certain where your paper will go. While you may have some general ideas, it's important to know what you want to say in each part of your paper before you start writing.

The zero draft lets you write to explore the topic and your ideas; the first draft is your first attempt at a coherent argument or explanation. When you write to explore, you are writing for yourself. When you write to argue or explain, you are writing for your audience; you have to demonstrate to your reader that you have read, thought about, understood, and processed the material.

## Free Writing

Surprisingly, not all the writing that you do has to be good. In fact, sometimes it's helpful to write without worrying about grammar, spelling, or punctuation. This is free writing: writing that is free from rules.

To free write, simply start writing about a topic or question—and don't stop. Put on a timer for a short, set amount of time and write to explore your ideas, topic concepts, or research results.

Your purpose is to develop your ideas about and your understanding of your subject. Free writing can help you identify flaws in your logic, missing evidence, or counter-arguments.

You may generate some great sentences in your free writing that you can use in your first draft. However, remember that free writing and writing your first draft are two separate things: they have different audiences and different purposes. It's best to keep the planning stage separate from the formal writing stage.

When free writing, don't worry about fixing mistakes. As long as *you* can understand what you've written, it's fine. If you are writing in a second language, feel free to include a word from your first language: you can look up the translation later. Remember, the focus is on generating and exploring ideas. With practice, you will learn to generate ideas more easily and will become a faster, more efficient writer.

## Journaling

Journaling is used to keep a record of what you did while preparing an assignment. Just as a diary helps you keep track of your personal life, a journal can help you keep track of your scholarly life—what you are reading, thinking, and learning.

Your journaling might include

- explorations of topics and key concepts (for assignments or for class)
- bibliographic information

- notes from classes and conversations with your instructor
- questions you would like to research
- ideas you have in class or while reading and studying
- new terminology

## Mind Mapping

Mind mapping allows you to explore your ideas while organizing them visually.

To create a mind map, write your topic or thesis statement in the middle of a page and write your main subtopics around it. Write ideas, arguments, quotes, and data under your subtopics. If you need to, further divide your topic and subtopics.

If you have too many ideas and are having trouble settling on a topic, create a mind map for each topic you think you might want to explore. This will help you to identify the best topic for an assignment.

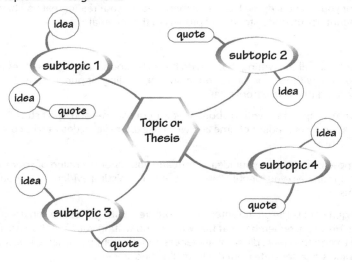

## Outlining

Many students dislike outlining. However, once you have a mind map, it's easy to create an outline. When you outline, you decide which ideas you are going to include in your paper and in what order. If you take time to develop your outline, you will end up knowing what you are going to include in each section and even paragraph of a paper. An outline can also help you identify which articles, textbooks, or readings you will need to have on hand as you write.

Outlining will lead to a clear first draft—and the more detailed your outline, the better. The stage of generating ideas has passed. You are now organizing what you want to say so that you can say it clearly.

By creating a linear, paragraph-by-paragraph plan, you simplify the writing process. Because you already know what is in each paragraph, writing the paragraphs becomes easier.

An outline starts with a specific thesis statement. It then explains the topic and evidence you will include in each paragraph or section. Here is a simple sample outline. (Note that the body of an essay doesn't have to contain three parts—it can have fewer or more—nor does each section need precisely three examples.)

**Sample outline**

Topic

The impact of higher tuition fees on university students

Thesis statement

Higher tuition fees not only damage university students' financial state but also affect their health and academic well-being.

Outline

1. Financial impacts

   1.1   Students have to work in order to support themselves financially.

   1.2   Students have less to spend on other things, including food, rent, and even personal hygiene.

   1.3   Students have to take out loans to cover their living costs.

2. Health implications

   2.1   The pressures of working and studying can lead to stress and in some cases substance abuse.

   2.2   Students may develop health problems from lack of sleep and poor nutrition.

   2.3   With little spare time, students can't exercise or pursue other healthy activities.

3. Academic consequences

   3.1   Students have to work more to earn a living and have less time to devote to their studies.

   3.2   Students are more likely to become ill and therefore miss classes, be late with assignments, and miss or do poorly on tests and exams.

   3.3   Some students drop out, change programs, or take fewer courses in order to work more.

This outline doesn't include the introduction or the conclusion, because at the planning stage you don't need to worry about them. If you think of a great way to start or end your assignment while still in the planning process, make note of it in your zero draft. This outline also does not include all the details you would want to include in your essay.

# THE MIDDLE 20: WRITING

Once you have finished planning, you are ready to start writing. In reality, the two stages are not completely separate; as you write, you will often find that you have to reconsider and revise your plans. You might need to do more mind mapping or revise your outline. However, at some point, you will be ready to put together a draft of your paper.

## Writing Your First Draft

In your first draft, you are putting together the pieces that you have already outlined, planned, and ordered. Because you are simply putting information together—not analyzing, revising, or second-guessing yourself—writing the first draft should take very little of the total time you spend working on an assignment.

Your first draft will not be your last draft, so you don't need to worry about whether it is perfect. Instead, focus on developing the ideas from your mind map and outline into sentences and paragraphs. You can highlight words that you don't feel are quite right or that you have repeated too often to remind yourself to revise them later. Or you can add a comment in the text to remind yourself of issues you need to deal with later. Using Track Changes in Word makes this easy to do.

When you are writing, work from your mind map and outline. Write one paragraph at a time. Try not to review what you have written until you have finished your first draft. Fight the temptation to tinker too early. Focus on getting your ideas into sentences and paragraphs. You will have lots of time to improve your writing when you move on to the editing stage.

## Difficulties Writers Face

If you have spent enough time planning, you will find that writing your first draft goes much more smoothly. However, some students still experience difficulties when it comes time to write. Here are some of the most common problems students face with the writing stage.

### Procrastination

If you procrastinate to avoid writing, you will find it works against you. Usually students put off writing because they think it will be too difficult. If this is the case for you, break your writing down into smaller chunks; it's easier to do one piece at a time.

If you procrastinate because you are unsure of what to write, you need to do more planning. If you procrastinate because you have run into a problem with your writing—a journal article that contradicts your thesis or confusion over your organization—give yourself time to think. In this case, sorting your sock drawer or doing laundry may be time well spent. As long as you are thinking and planning, you're not actually procrastinating—you're preparing yourself to sit down and write.

### Perfectionism

You may feel that your writing is basic and your knowledge imperfect. It can be daunting to start writing if your goal is a perfect product. It's important to remember that no writing is perfect. You could spend days perfecting your sentences—and many famous writers do—but, it's likely that you would still make the odd mistake.

As a student, you probably don't have days to pore over your writing. You may have a stack of other assignments on your desk that also need your attention. You have to do the best you can in the time you have. Trying to do more will only cause you stress.

If you are really worried about your writing, talk to a tutor or your instructor. You don't have to take their advice, but it can help to talk to others about your work.

### Writer's Block

Writer's block can be a stifling, frustrating experience, especially if you have multiple assignments with looming deadlines. Reading and writing about your topic should allow you to compile a sizeable zero draft. Putting your ideas into an outline will give you a solid foundation for your draft. If you have fully engaged in the planning activities described in the previous section, you should be able to overcome writer's block. After all, if you have done enough planning, you should know exactly what it is you are going to write—now you just have to write it.

If you are having trouble getting words down on the page even though you have planned carefully, take a break. Do something that frees your mind from what you have to do, then try again.

### Lack of Confidence

You might have concluded, somewhere in your schooling, that you can't write well, that it's not even worth trying. Even if you have always struggled as a writer, it doesn't mean that you will always struggle. You might have to develop new writing habits, including planning and editing your writing. You might have to spend more time learning English grammar so that your instructor can more clearly understand what you are trying to say. Use the feedback you have received on previous assignments and your knowledge of how you approach your assignments to determine what makes you a "poor" writer. With this knowledge of your writing weaknesses, you can develop a plan to become a better writer.

### Fear of Writing

Writing can be stressful and, for some students, even painful, but it doesn't have to be. If you put enough time into planning your writing, you should be able to narrow the gap between what you are trying to say and what you write. If the very thought of writing fills you with dread, remember that the key to controlling the process is to plan what you are going to say before you start writing.

## THE FINAL 40: REVISING AND EDITING

The final stage of the writing process is when you turn your first draft into a complete and polished paper, ready to hand in. Like the planning stage, the revising stage should take about forty percent of the time you spend on a writing assignment. Together, these two stages are what will make the greatest difference in the quality of your finished product.

Revising your own work can be challenging. When we look at our own writing, we often see what we *think* is on the page rather than what is actually there. However, with time and practice, you can learn how to edit your own drafts. Becoming a good self-editor will enable you to

- catch errors that could confuse or irritate the reader
- check that your organization is sound

- learn about your own writing and what you need to improve
- clean up problems that you didn't address in your draft (grammar, punctuation, word choice, repetition, transitions, and other oversights and errors)

## Questions to Use When You Edit

As you read through your draft, use the following questions to identify what needs to be revised. Some questions will lead to minor revisions; others might require you to rethink your approach, revise your argument, or rewrite sentences, paragraphs, or whole sections of a paper. You might have to do more research or reread articles to clarify your thinking. By closely examining every aspect of your draft, you will discover what you still need to do to improve it.

- Does my paper fulfill the requirements of the assignment?
- Is my thesis statement clear?
- Is my argument supported by clearly stated evidence?
- Is my paper well organized?
- Does each paragraph have a topic sentence?
- Does each paragraph support my thesis?
- Have I cited sources correctly?
- Are my sentences clear and concise?
- Have I varied my sentence structure?
- Have I checked for repetition?
- Is my grammar correct?
- Is my spelling correct?
- Is my punctuation correct?

## Strategies for Successful Editing

### Switch Assignments

If you have trouble editing your own work, try working with others. Switch assignments with classmates and have them critique your writing. They may be able to point out things you would have missed.

When you receive your paper back, read through any feedback. Discuss it. It can be enlightening to learn how a reader views your writing. You also gain valuable writing and editing skills when you edit someone else's writing. Soon you should be able to transfer those editing skills to your own writing.

### Try a Different Medium

Don't revise your writing on the computer screen every time you look at it. Print out your document and read through it with a pen, highlighters, and sticky notes. Write notes to yourself. Highlight problem sentences.

## Take it Slow

Focus on one thing at a time. For example, start with assessing the argument your paper makes. Examine transitions. Check for subject-verb agreement. Look for spelling errors.

## Check Your Argument

Highlight your thesis statement and your topic sentences. Do the topic sentences support the thesis statement? Is there a clear topic sentence for each paragraph? Does everything in each paragraph relate to its topic?

## Work Backwards

Make a post-outline: Read through your paper to draw out the important points. Then use these important points to form an outline. If you used an outline in the planning process, does your post-outline differ? If so, why? Should it be different? If you didn't start with an outline, does your post-outline match what it is you think your paper should be saying?

## Read Aloud

Read your writing out loud. You'd be surprised how many grammatical mistakes and awkward sentences you can catch by doing this. Try reading your paper backwards: start with the last sentence; then read the second-to-last sentence. By reversing the order of the sentences you can easily focus on grammar and punctuation instead of the ideas the paragraph is expressing.

## Take Time Out

Don't edit your draft right after you have written it. Give yourself some time before you edit it so you can see it with fresh eyes. It is easier to be critical of something if you haven't just spent hours writing it.

If this doesn't work, trick your brain by reading random paragraphs or changing the physical position of your body. Any of these strategies will help you can gain a fresh perspective on overly familiar work.

## Compare

Read some writing—an article or academic book—that you thought was particularly good. Now compare it to your own. How do the two differ? If the other piece is better than yours, what makes it better? Can you use any of the strategies the author has used? Are there good transitional words or phrases (*moreover, therefore, however, in spite of, because of*, and so forth) that could improve your writing or the flow of ideas in your paper? You can learn a lot by assessing others' writing and applying what you learn to your own writing.

## Check It

Use a checklist to assess your writing. If you were given a rubric against which your assignment will be marked, use it to evaluate your writing. If you were not given a rubric or an assignment checklist, ask your instructor what he or she will look for when marking the assignments, or return to the list of questions above and use it as a checklist.

# Reading Academic Writing

## WHY READING MATTERS

Academic writing is generally considered the most advanced and demanding skill that students must master at university. However, it is academic reading that is actually the core skill upon which good academic writing depends. It is through reading that you acquire new vocabulary, absorb new ways of using language, and learn to think deeply and critically about ideas—all skills that you will need as an academic writer.

Becoming a strong academic reader—and thus a strong academic writer—requires three key skills:

- **the ability to read actively:** to comprehend, absorb, and retain what you read
- **the ability to read critically:** to analyze, evaluate, synthesize, and interpret what you read
- **the ability to read fluently:** to recognize most words that you read and learn the meanings of those you don't

The following guidelines will help you become a stronger and more efficient academic reader.

## READING ACTIVELY

There is more to reading than just skimming the page and jotting down a quote that seems like it might impress your instructor. Reading, especially at the university level, is an active process that requires you to concentrate, check your understanding, and record important details from your reading. Reading actively will improve both your comprehension of and your ability to retain and recall what you read. It will also help build your documentation skills, as you observe how authors incorporate and document the ideas of others in their writing.

Here are some strategies for becoming an active reader.

### Pre-reading

Before you begin to read, free write on the topic to identify what you already know and feel about it. Think about your exisiting knowledge of the topic as well as any related experiences you've had and views you hold. Pre-reading is a crucial first step to avoid being dominated by the "authorities" you're currently reading—so that you don't end up simply thinking other people's thoughts.

### Annotating

When you **annotate** a text, you mark up, highlight, and make notes on the page as you read. Annotating as you go means you won't have to read the entire text again in the future—you can simply refer to your annotations and reread relevant sections. Annotating in this way will also help you retain and recall what you have read, which is useful when you are writing essays and exams.

Remember that highlighting and underlining are only useful if accompanied by notes that indicate the significance of what is highlighted. Don't highlight more than is necessary; if you highlight the entire article, the exercise is pointless.

## Note-taking

When you **note-take**, you record details from your reading to check your understanding and to use in the future, perhaps as a study aid or in your own writing. As you research, it is useful to record the main points of an article, the author's name, and the publication information in a journal or notebook (electronic or print). Your notes will help you remember and understand the main points of the reading and will direct you to important passages you may want to quote from or refer to in your writing.

Not all note-taking has to take the form of written prose. You may find it helpful to create outlines or concept maps to record important ideas from your reading. Use whichever methods help you record your understanding in a way that is decipherable in case you need your notes for future reference.

## Identifying Key Information

Annotating and note-taking are useful strategies only if they help you to absorb and retain the information you need from a text. To do that, you have to pay attention to certain key features of the text as you read.

**Thesis.** The thesis is the main claim or point the author is making in a piece. Sometimes this statement is clear and explicit; sometimes, it is implied or otherwise hard to figure out. If so, take the time to make sense of the argument. It is the most important part of a text.

**Significant claims.** Significant supporting claims or arguments are almost as important as the thesis. These are often found in topic sentences. Underlining or restating these claims in notes as you read can help you understand the author's purpose and follow the author's argument.

**Key terms and unfamiliar words.** If an author uses a particular word or phrase repeatedly, it is likely important to understanding the essay. Highlight or underline such words and phrases. Be certain that you not only understand what the word or phrase means in general but what it means in the context of the essay. Look up any words that are unfamiliar.

**Important ideas.** Marking important ideas within a text will help you to piece together its meaning. Linking these ideas together will help you to establish the logic and structure of a piece. Paraphrasing these ideas—writing them down in your own words—can help you understand the text, as well as recall the ideas at a later point.

**Memorable passages or images.** Sometimes, passages or images in a text stand out and seem important. Noting why they may be important will help you understand their function. Referring to these ideas within your own work can help to make your own writing more memorable.

**Questions and comments.** Writing down your questions and comments can help you think critically about the text. Note places where an idea is unclear or calls into question the premises or claims asserted by the author. You can also write down ideas that you think should be explored further or have been missed. They can make excellent essay topics or subtopics for your own papers.

# READING CRITICALLY

After you have read through a text actively at least once and are confident you understand what you have read, you are ready to read it critically. To read critically is not necessarily to criticize. It means you should ask questions about a text and carefully examine its claims. Is there another way you could look at the topic? Is every point the author makes supported by evidence? Is the evidence correct and properly cited? Are there flaws in the author's logic? How does this article compare with the one you read yesterday on the same topic? How and why do they differ?

## Becoming a Good Critical Reader

**Read thoroughly.** Take the time to read thoroughly and with concentration. Pay attention to the details. You don't want to miss a large chunk of information simply because you were reading too quickly. You need to understand what an author is saying about a topic before voicing an opinion on it. That way, you can defend your opinion with relevant information.

**Dig deeper.** Curiosity, wanting to know why things are the way they are or how they work, leads us to ask important questions. If you are interested in knowing more about a subject, read more about it. Find out the *why* and the *how*. Perhaps it will lead you somewhere you never expected to go.

**Question what you read.** A healthy dose of skepticism will do wonders for your research. If Einstein had happily accepted the theories that had already been put forward, he wouldn't have written his theories of relativity. When you are reading, it is a good idea to ask whether you agree with the arguments being made. You might have reason to question. If you are unsure about the validity of something, research it further. Maybe you were right to question. Just because something is published doesn't mean it is truth or fact—it just means it was printed on paper or posted online.

**Keep track of the author's argument.** Pay attention to what authors say and what they said they would say in an argument. Are there gaps in the argument? Do they make leaps from fact to assertion without enough support? Is the information they are using as evidence accurate? Is it outdated? Is it theoretical? Did they tell you everything they said they would? Is the evidence based on primary or secondary sources? Is it based on credible research? Analyze what is being said as you read and after you read. Reread if necessary. If you think something important is missing, it probably is.

**Develop new questions.** As you read, questions should naturally arise. Pay attention to those questions. Write them down. By asking questions and allowing yourself to acknowledge them when they arise, you will be better able to examine and engage with your reading.

# KEEPING TRACK OF WHAT YOU READ

When you research for a class, for a project or assignment, or for personal interest, you will probably look at a variety of different materials and sources. You might read several journal articles, an e-book or two, some essays, and a few chapters from books in the library; you might discuss your research with an instructor. When you are taking several university-level courses and reading articles every day of the week, all of the information you take in can become jumbled.

There is hope, however. Here are some tips for easily keeping track of what you read.

## Keeping Track of Sources

There are several ways to keep track of your sources. You can keep notes or a journal, recording what you've read. You can keep files of photocopies and printouts. You can bookmark a file electronically. Or you can use a mix of all these methods. No matter which method you use, it is a good idea to record the following information:

### When You Read the Article

Write down the date on which you read an article, especially if the article is online, as the content of websites can shift and change.

### Where You Read the Article

Keep track of where you found the article. Write down the website, the page, the chapter, the name of the journal. Wherever the information is, you may need to find it again or cite it.

### Who Wrote the Article

In addition to the author's name, record any observations about the author or source: Is the author or source credible? Has the author or source produced any other articles on the subject? Is the research current? You might want to look up other articles by a specific author, and you might have to find another, more credible source for specific information.

### When the Article Was Written and Where It Was Published

Be sure to record all publication information. You will need it when you document your sources. You might also need to find a more current edition, want to find more recent information, or wish to compare two editions at some point.

### What Type of Source It Is

Is it a book? A file folder? A transcript of an interview with a professor? A website? An online journal article? Know what your source is so that you can easily locate it and easily reference it if you need to.

## Keeping Notes

It's easy to keep a few pages in your binder or notebook where you write down important readings for your classes. You can organize entries by the date you read an article, by the author's name, by the type of source, by the information you were looking for, or by the location of the article. Below are some examples of ways you could write down a source:

> Library, Basement Level, Moveable Shelf De–Ds. Book. De Silva, Haviar. *Riding Your Horse Elegantly*. Ch. 2: Sitting Positions, p. 16–18. Publisher: Browne and Cummings: Sao Paulo, 1852. Read 12/06/2010. (Information on how a lady should sit on her horse.)

> Feminine horse-riding positions in nineteenth-century Brazil—diagrams. Book. De Silva, Haviar. *Riding Your Horse Elegantly*. Browne and Cummings: Sao Paulo, 1852. See chapter 2, pages 16 to 18. Read on June 12.

> De Silva, Haviar. *Riding Your Horse Elegantly*. "The Female and the Saddle." Browne and Cummings: Sao Paulo, 1852. (June 12)

> 12 June 2010. *Riding Your Horse Elegantly*. Haviar de Silva. Browne and Cummings: Sao Paulo, 1852. (p 16, 17, 18); in library basement

## Using Bookmarks

If you bookmark sites that you think you might need for academic projects, be careful not to end up with a long, unmanageable list that will make no sense to you three weeks after you compiled it. Create folders for specific courses or projects. Include sub-folders organized by topic. By organizing yourself as you research, you will save yourself time later, when you are in a rush to find sources or information you know you've read somewhere.

Check the help section of your Internet browser for further guidance on how to create and organize bookmarks.

# BUILDING YOUR ACADEMIC VOCABULARY

The vocabulary you will encounter in your reading at university can be challenging— and is meant to be. The new words your studies introduce you to represent the new knowledge you are acquiring. You will learn terminology specific to your discipline, whether it is chemistry or nursing, as well as new words that represent the advanced concepts you will be studying.

Your success in your studies depends largely on your ability to understand what you are reading. The words you miss or skip because they are unfamiliar represent gaps in your understanding of what you read. Expanding your vocabulary will make your academic reading more efficient and, in turn, will make you a better, more precise academic writer.

## Read Widely

The best way to build your vocabulary is also the easiest way: by reading. When you read, you unconsciously absorb new words and new contexts for or meanings of familiar words. It doesn't matter so much what you read as long as you read and as long as what you read is challenging and diverse.

■ **Read constantly**—books, websites, magazines, newspapers. Read for your studies, read for interest, and read for entertainment. Look for authors you enjoy, in both fiction and non-fiction. The more reading you do and the more varied your reading, the larger and more versatile your vocabulary will be.

■ **Challenge yourself.** Push yourself to read types of writing that are out of your usual pattern of reading or that take effort. If the reading you are doing is easy, you probably aren't learning much from it.

■ **Read about new topics.** The more popular the topic, the more limited the vocabulary is likely to be. Your favourite online magazine might be brilliantly written, but if you are reading about the same things—no matter how specialized—you aren't likely to encounter many new words.

## Look for Context Clues

When you encounter an unfamiliar word in your reading, before heading for a dictionary, try to figure out the meaning from the clues in the text that surrounds it. This strategy is by far the easiest way to learn new words and is the way you have learned most of the words you know now.

■ **Take a guess at what the word is likely to mean.** Often you can come close to understanding a word simply by considering what it probably means. Consider the sentence "While jurors were promised a six-month break, their hiatus was abruptly cancelled when the judge ordered the trial to resume." Even without knowing the precise meaning of *hiatus*, you can guess from the rest of the sentence that it is referring to a break or interruption, which is exactly what it means.

■ **Look for definitions included in the text.** Often a definition is built into the same sentence as the new word. Notice the definition in the following sentence: "The roots of the fast-growing poplar tree take up soil contaminants in a process called *phytoremediation*." Definitions of this kind are usually indicated by *referred to as, called,* or simply *is.*

■ **Carefully read what comes before and after** the sentence in which the new word appears to see if the meaning becomes clear by the way the ideas unfold. You may have to keep reading well beyond the word before it will become clear, but often the larger context in which the word appears holds clues to its meaning.

## Learn Word Roots

Although English is considered a Germanic language, its academic vocabulary is built mainly from Latin and Greek roots. Learning these roots, as well as suffixes (word endings), and prefixes (word beginnings), can help you decode many unfamiliar academic words.

For a list of common word roots, prefixes, and suffixes, see page 167.

## Use a Dictionary

Looking words up in a dictionary is the best way to check your understanding of a word or to determine its exact meaning. The dictionary also provides much more information about a word, which may strengthen or help clarify your understanding. The dictionary entry for a word shows

- all meanings of the word
- any variant spellings (for example, *analyze/analyse; sulfur/sulphur*)
- whether the word is capitalized or hyphenated
- the word's origin
- the word's part of speech
- how the word is pronounced

Depending on the dictionary you use, it may also provide synonyms, antonyms, and examples of the word's usage.

If you use an online dictionary, be sure it is one that provides all the information listed above. If it is an American dictionary (as most are), be aware that it will show Canadian and British spellings only as variants. As a student, you likely have access, through your libraries' website, to online versions of the *Canadian Oxford Dictionary,* the complete *Oxford English Dictionary*, and dual-language dictionaries in many languages.

## Strengthen Your Understanding

To make a new word part of your active vocabulary, it is important to do more than look up its meaning. Keep a notebook or list of new words and their definitions. For pronunciation help, use an online dictionary to hear the word spoken. Read the dictionary entry and then try to put the definition in your own words. Note any words that are derived from the word (for example, if you look up *reliable*, you will find *reliability, reliably, unreliable* and other derived words). Try to write an original sentence that uses the word as you understand it. And most importantly, *use it*. Say it and write it as much as possible so that you remember it.

# Researching

Much of what you will do as a student requires research; it is one of the central activities at universities, for both students and faculty. Whether you are writing an essay on the Stroop effect, preparing a report on how to reduce traffic congestion in Victoria, comparing the employment opportunities of new Canadians with those of people born in Canada, or studying how anaerobic bacteria are used to treat sewage, research is central to your success as a learner, a reader, and a learner.

The term *research* can apply to many things; we can research anything from our family history to a new car. But research, as the term is used in universities, has a more narrow definition. Academic research refers to the systematic search for answers to specific, original questions in order to create new knowledge.

To become an effective researcher, you need a number of skills: reading and writing, most of all, but also the ability to ask good research questions, to search for and gather information efficiently, to apply a critical perspective to information, to use the conventions of documentation, and to analyze, interpret, synthesize, and evaluate what you have read and learned.

Many of these skills are covered elsewhere in this guide.

- For advice on effective reading, refer to ""Reading Academic Writing" on page 22.
- For advice on writing a research paper, refer to "Writing a Research Paper" on page 101.
- For advice on incorporating sources, refer to ""Using Sources" on page 40.

In this section, you will find advice on defining good research topics and questions, developing a research plan, finding information, online and elsewhere, and evaluating your sources. You can find more advice on researching through your university library.

If you are doing a major research project, you will find it worthwhile to invest in a good research guide that is written specifically for your discipline. Ask your instructor or a librarian for suggestions—or, better yet, do your own research! Refer to your university's library website, which should provide a thorough overview of research topics and tips, or look online, where you will also find a wealth of information and guidance, including advice specific to the type of research you are doing and to your discipline.

## DEFINING A GOOD RESEARCH TOPIC

Every research project has to start somewhere—and that starting point is the research topic. You may have been given your topic or some guidelines on acceptable topics, or you may be free to pick your own topic. Whichever the case, you will need to focus your topic before you go any further.

To move from the general to the specific, take the topic apart. It is best to do this by asking questions and doing some preliminary research, such as an Internet search. (Note: Although Wikipedia is not considered a reliable source of information, it can guide you to specific sources and orient you in your search for information.)

Example    You have chosen to write about fish farming. You look up fish farming on Google and look at what types of fish farming exist, what sort of fish are farmed, why fish are farmed, where fish are farmed, and the impacts of fish farming. As you explore these ideas, you begin to see some specific topics within the general topic of fish farming, such as the following:

- salmon farming and the spread of sea lice among wild salmon
- pollution from salmon farming: the impact of salmon-farming waste on the environment
- trout farming as an efficient and environmentally sound protein source

The preliminary thinking and researching you do will help you identify what, exactly, you want to research.

## Tips for Choosing a Research Topic

**Understand your research task.** Be clear about what you have been asked to do. Read through your assignment and any instructions that might help you decide on a suitable topic.

**Follow your interests.** If permitted, select a topic that interests you. The easiest topics to work with are ones you find exciting and are motivated to learn about. Also, think about what knowledge might benefit you in your career or in your community. Each research paper provides you with the opportunity to further not only your reading, researching, and writing skills but also your knowledge in a particular field.

**Generate ideas.** Whether you have chosen a topic or it has been chosen for you, use a concept map or other brainstorming method to generate all the ideas you can about your topic. You can continue to add to your concept map as you learn more about your topic.

**Explore.** Do some preliminary research to see where your ideas take you. An initial Internet search will likely turn up possibilities that you haven't considered. Discuss your ideas with classmates, friends, instructors, or a librarian.

**Narrow your topic.** Use your explorations to settle on a topic that is clear, specific, and meets the requirements of your assignment.

**Keep moving forward.** Deciding on a topic can be hard, especially when you begin a research project. It is easy to keep trying out new ideas, but you can waste a lot of time that way. Sometimes, you just have to force yourself to stick with a topic and move forward with it.

## DEFINING A GOOD RESEARCH QUESTION

Once you have your topic, you may feel that you are set to go. But a research topic alone will not lead you to the answers that a good research project should produce. For that, you need a focused research question. Without a question, you may find yourself overwhelmed by the information you gather on your topic. The only way you can know which information you need is to limit your search with one or more research questions. A good research question is the key to successful research.

Consider the fish farming example above. Starting with a narrowed topic, you can formulate questions that will make your research process more efficient. At first, it can be hard to know what questions to ask: the ability to ask good questions—like most abilities—comes with practice. The best place to start is to take apart your (now more specific) topic.

Example   If you have chosen to write about trout farming as an efficient and environmentally sound protein source, examine the terms within the topic. How are trout farmed? How are other fish farmed? How does trout farming differ from, for example, salmon farming? Are trout easy to farm? What sort of threats to the environment does trout farming pose? Can those threats be minimized? How can they be minimized? What is an efficient, environmentally sound practice? How is trout farming efficient and environmentally sound? How is it not? Where are trout usually farmed? Why are trout a good source of protein? What other sources of protein are there? How do the farming practices of other sources of protein (chicken, beef, soy) compare with trout farming? Are they more or less efficient and environmentally sound?

Once you have brainstormed a set of questions about your topic, check to see whether they capture what you want to know. A good question should lead to new knowledge or a new way of looking at an issue. Avoid questions that require simple information retrieval (for example, How much trout do trout farms produce?). A good question should lead to an answer based on evidence. Avoid questions that can only be guessed at (for example, Are farmed trout happier than wild trout?). Organize your questions to see which ones overlap or can be combined into a larger question.

You can see how questions will help you identify what, exactly, you are trying to find out. Sometimes, your questions will lead you to realize that the topic you believed at first to be specific was not quite specific enough, and you will need to narrow it more, ideally to a single focused question. In the trout farming example, you might end up with a question like this: *Which is a more environmentally sustainable protein source: farmed trout or soy?* Your research could then lead to a research paper comparing the food benefits and environmental costs of the two protein sources.

## DEVELOPING A RESEARCH PLAN

Once you have developed your topic and questions, your next step is to create a research plan. A plan, whether detailed or bare-bones, will help you figure out the steps you need to take and ensure that you allow yourself enough time to complete them all. Good research takes time, and without a plan, it is easy to end up trying to do everything at the last minute.

Here are some guidelines for creating a research plan:

**Decide which questions you will answer.** Which questions are the most important to your research? You may not have enough time to explore them all. Is there some information that is hard to find and is central to your argument? Try to deal with hard-to-do and have-to-do aspects of your search before anything else. They may take more time than you expect them to.

**Brainstorm search strategies.** Beside each question you wish to answer, write down several ideas of where you might find the answer. It is less frustrating to be unable to find what you are looking for if you have an idea about where to look next. Check the list of potential sources (below) that go beyond simple Internet searches and the university library. If all else fails, ask an expert where you should look; an instructor or a librarian may have an idea of where you can find the information you seek.

**Link expected results to your topic.** Do the results you are expecting to find serve your purpose? Do they support your argument? Ensure that everything you are looking for is related to your overall goal. Will the information you want help you to answer a reader's questions or is it simply interesting trivia? Make sure that you aren't looking for information that you don't need and that will clutter your essay.

**Organize your research.** Traditional methods of keeping track of what you find, like keeping note cards, have largely been replaced by more efficient, digital methods. Whatever method you use, the goal is to record and organize your information so that you can keep track of it efficiently. Your system should allow you to identify every source you use in your writing.

Tools that will let you bookmark and tag web pages come with most Internet browsers. Spend a few minutes doing the tutorial on the use of these tools in your favourite browser so that you know how to use them when you start.

The **Firefox** browser features two free extensions that can be very useful in keeping track of your research: **Diigo** is a social networking tool that allows you to bookmark and tag web pages and add sticky notes; **Zotero** is a powerful citation manager that allows you to annotate web pages. It also generates citations in whatever citation style you choose. Both take only a few minutes to learn and have good tutorials.

In addition to using bookmarks and tags, many researchers keep a file on their computer in which they can paste URLs, keep notes about particular pages they've visited, and record other notes about a project.

## FINDING SOURCES

Understanding the different types of research sources will help you research efficiently. Knowing what sources exist will help you decide where to look first—a government statistics website, an online newspaper archive, a journal database—to find the information you seek.

### Types of Sources

**Primary sources** are original sources of information produced by those who created, experienced, witnessed, or recorded the information. Primary sources include letters, journals, eyewitness accounts, research data, photos, sound recordings, and artifacts. In literature, primary sources include the novels, poems, and other types of writing that are studied. In science, they are experimental results or studies.

**Secondary sources** are the products of research using primary sources. Secondary sources include studies, books, and other products of scholarly research. Secondary sources interpret, analyze, evaluate, or otherwise use primary sources for the purposes of research.

**Tertiary sources** provide information that is distilled or synthesized from secondary sources. Encyclopedias, including Wikipedia, are tertiary sources. They can be very useful as a starting point for exploring a topic or finding out the state of knowledge about a topic, but they are not considered scholarly sources, and your instructor may not accept their use in assignments.

In addition to primary, secondary, and tertiary sources, academic research also distinguishes between **scholarly** and **popular** sources. While both can be useful sources of information, most academic research relies on scholarly sources. Your instructor may specify whether you must use scholarly sources only or whether popular sources are acceptable. If you still aren't sure, ask your instructor for guidance.

**Scholarly sources** include books and journals written by academics for other academics and students. These are the sources that have the greatest reliability and authority. Journal articles are usually peer-reviewed, meaning they have been reviewed by other academics. Scholarly sources contain full documentation of their own research sources, and present new research and knowledge about their topic.

**Popular sources** include magazines, newspapers, websites, and other print or online publications. They are written by non-academics, including journalists, professional writers, and other writers. They generally do not cite their sources, may contain advertising, and cover a wide range of subjects of interest to their readers.

## KNOWING WHERE AND HOW TO LOOK

The quality of the research you do depends directly on how skilled you are at finding answers to your research questions. While a simple Internet search is easy and will often return more results than you could ever read, it can be highly inefficient. If your search terms aren't narrow enough, or if you give up reading the results after a few pages, you can easily miss the information you were looking for.

As part of developing your research plan, consider where the answers you are looking for are likely to be. While a search engine, like Google, is now the starting point for most people who are looking for information, there are sources beyond Google that you should consider. Some of these have the advantage of containing information that Google does not; others have the advantage of being a more efficient way of locating information than through Google.

Some information you are looking for is not in digital form; if it is, it may not be indexed by Google or other search engines, so your search will not find it. Other information can be found more efficiently by different search strategies. For example, subject directories organize information by topic, making it possible to go more directly to what you are looking for.

The following are some of the most useful resources and tools to make your searching more efficient.

### Library Resources

Whatever your research topic or questions, the library is the place to start. Libraries are not just home to much of the information you will be using in your research—they are also the place to learn about researching. Most university libraries offer tutorials on using their card and online catalogues, online databases (including EBSCO, JSTOR, PubMed, Elsevier Science, and others), newspaper indexes, archives, and other sources.

Most university libraries, and often even local libraries, include a vast collection of resources, including

- print books and e-books, accessible through the library catalogues or in the stacks
- print and online references, including online dictionaries, thesauruses, and other reference volumes
- print and online periodicals, such as scholarly journals and newspapers from all over the world
- journal databases, including all the major databases and many specialized and discipline-specific databases
- statistical databases, including all Statistics Canada data and other paid statistical database subscriptions
- audio-visual resources, including scores, CDs, and videos
- special collections, including rare books, manuscripts, photographs, and oral histories
- archival materials, including valuable historical records

Best of all, libraries have librarians who can help you with your questions about research. Subject librarians can provide in-depth research help in specific areas of study and are available in person and, in some cases, online.

## Academic Databases

As mentioned above, your university library website offers access to many online databases of scholarly sources as well as e-tutorials in how to use them effectively. Much of your academic writing will require you to use scholarly sources, so becoming competent in the use of academic databases is an important research skill to master. Instructions for searching these databases are not included in this guide, but you will find clear, thorough tutorials through your library website.

## Google Tools

Google's basic search engine is so easy to use and so powerful that it's easy to overlook Google's other tools. Google allows you to limit your search to a specific type of source, using the following tools:

- **advanced search:** an advanced search allows you to limit your search to specific file types, filter pages with unwanted terms, or search within a specific domain
- **images:** a Google Image search will return photos, maps, diagrams, visual art, or any other illustration of your keyword
- **books:** Google Books archives many whole and partial books, including old, rare, and out-of-print volumes; you can set the advanced search so that it returns only full texts or partial texts
- **scholarly sources:** Google Scholar will find journal articles, abstracts, theses, and books for you in many disciplines

- **news:** Google News lets you search for current news stories from around the world; Google News Archive allows you to search news archives for much of the past century

Google also allows you to search in a specific language or translate pages into another language.

Google also suggests *related searches*, which can often help you narrow your search by presenting the most common searches related to your search term.

The key to using Google effectively is to learn about the advanced methods of searching its billions of pages. Even a few minutes invested in learning how to use its advanced features will save you much time and effort.

## Google Search Tips

The following tips are adapted with permission from the University of Victoria Libraries' website:

Before searching in Google using plain language, consider crafting your search with specific techniques to retrieve more relevant results.

**Omit "and":** *and* is implied in Google searches and therefore is not necessary.

Separate searches for [environmental policy] and [environmental AND policy] will retrieve the same results.

**Use quotation marks (" ")** to limit your search to a specific phase.

["climate change"] will search for results with this exact phase. A search for [climate change] will search for results with instances of both the words *climate* and *change*, and retrieve such unrelated results as "The political climate has changed since the adoption of free trade."

**OR** can be used to search using multiple words that express a similar concept. OR must be capitalized so Google understands it as a searching word, not a word to be searched.

For example, [teenager OR adolescent OR youth]

["climate change" OR "global warming"]

**Use "-" to exclude pages** that contain a specified word. Type the minus sign immediately before the word you want to exclude. (Don't put a space between the minus sign and the term.)

[fish farming -salmon] will retrieve pages about fish farming other than salmon farming.

**Pay attention to word order**.

[Genetic engineering] and [engineering genetics] will retrieve different results.

**Use an asterisk (*),** also called a wild card, to retrieve words with multiple endings.

Canad* will retrieve Canada, Canadian, and Canadians

feminis* will retrieve feminism, feminisms, feminist, and feminists

**Use the tilde (~)** to search for synonyms and to help you locate words with similar meanings. (The tilde symbol is found to the left of the number keys on most keyboards.)

> [~car] will retrieve automobile, vehicle

**Set limits** to Google searches. Here are some common terms that can be used to limit your search:

> **intitle:** retrieves search words which appear in the website's title field; for example, [intitle:canad* "climate change"] will return pages that have any form of "Canada" or "Canadian" and "climate change" in their title.

> **inurl:** retrieves search words which appear in the websites's URL; for example, [inurl:shakespeare "elizabethan england"] will return pages that have these terms in their URL.

> **filetype:** retrieves specific file types such as HTML, PDFs, Word (doc), Excel (xls), or PowerPoint (ppt); for example, [filetype:pdf "organizational development"] will return PDFs that contain the phrase "organizational development."

## Wikipedia

Like Google, Wikipedia has become a first stop for many students faced with a research project. It can be a useful tertiary source, just as an encyclopedia can help you learn enough about a subject to clarify your understanding and help you narrow a topic. But the use of Wikipedia often comes with a warning about its reliability, largely because the articles are anonymous and because anyone can edit the articles. Some instructors ask their students to add inaccurate information to Wikipedia articles just to show how easily it can be done.

Wikipedia does, however, have some important advantages. It provides (often detailed) coverage of specialized topics that may otherwise be hard to research, such as information about local events from around the world. Because of its large base of contributors, articles are continuously updated, providing information that would not be available in other sources for months or years. It also provides links to other Wikipedia articles on related subjects and to websites that were used as sources, some of which may be more reliable sources of information.

It is best to treat Wikipedia as a source of ideas about a topic. Use the articles to get a general understanding of your topic, but always verify the information with a more reliable, scholarly source. Best of all, use the links listed as references as a starting point for further research.

## Subject Directories

Subject directories allow you to find information by category rather than by search term. They use a tree structure, starting with several major categories that branch into subcategories that grow progressively more refined. For example, if you were using Open Directory, one of the largest subject directories, to research sleep disorders, you would start by choosing "Health" at the top level, followed by "Conditions and Diseases" and then "Sleep Disorders," where you would find a list of sleep disorders and links to pages and sites dealing with sleep disorders.

The advantage of subject directories is that they limit your search results to a manageable number and lead you directly to sites that deal with your topic. Because subject directories are compiled by humans instead of computers, they can be more focused and reliable than search engines. Scholarly subject directories, like INFOMINE and Intute, can be particularly useful in limiting and focusing your search results, saving you time otherwise spent scrolling through many pages of Google results. These subject directories now use keyword searching as well, so they combine the power of a search engine and the convenience of a subject directory. INFOMINE also allows you to refine your search by many criteria, including academic discipline and resource type (such as abstract or electronic journal).

## Government Websites

All levels of government in Canada have well-developed websites or portals where you can find information about government policies and programs, as well as publications, data, and sometimes forms. Governments around the world offer similar services. Government websites may contain information that is not indexed by search engines and so cannot be found through a Google search.

Provincial and municipal government websites can be found by searching by name. The following are some of the government websites of national interest:

■ The **Canada Site** is the website of the Canadian federal government. It provides information on the government's programs and services, organized by ministry and by category of information.

■ The **Archives Canada** website is the official portal for the Canadian federal archives as well as for eight hundred other archives from across Canada. From the main website, you can link to provincial and territorial archives, university archives, medical archives, and religious archives.

■ The **Statistics Canada** website publishes statistical data on a wide range of topics and is organized by type of reader, including analysts and researchers. Some data are available by paid subscription only, but most universities allow their students access to the Statistics Canada database through their libraries' website.

## Internet Archive

The **Internet Archive** is a digital library that offers storage and access to billions of websites, current and past, as well as digitized books, music, and images. Among its projects are the **Open Library**, which contains 1.6 million free downloadable books; **Moving Image**, a collection of films, newsreels, cartoons, and other movies; and **Audio Archive**, a collection of music, broadcasts, radio shows, and audio books, including over 50,000 concert recordings. Through its **Wayback Machine**, you can search over 150 billion archived websites dating back to the early days of the World Wide Web. The Wayback Machine offers archived versions of the Web, allowing users to see previous versions of websites or to visit web pages that no longer exist. Through it, you will be able to find articles that have since been deleted.

## Invisible Internet

If you have come to expect that everything you might want to find is only a Google search away, think again. Only a small portion of all web pages are indexed by search engines and are therefore findable by them. The majority of web pages are part of what is called the invisible or deep web. Most of the content that is invisible to search engines is in private intranets (networks within organizations), sites requiring registration or login, archives (such as those maintained by newspapers), PDF files that can't be searched for by keywords, and what are called dynamic web pages, web pages that are created only for a specific viewing (such as an airline reservation). While many of these pages are of little research interest, there are cases where you may be searching for something specific—a government report, for example—that will be invisible to your search engine.

Several websites claim to be able to search the invisible web. You can find them by Googling "invisible web." In some cases, you may find the document at the main website (many government documents in PDF format can be searched for and accessed from the government's web page). In other cases, you may have to get help from a librarian, who will be able to tell you where the information you are looking for is likely to be found.

## EVALUATING SOURCES

Just because something is published or printed does not make it accurate, reliable, or correct. Online sources in particular, because of the democratic nature of the Internet, have to be evaluated carefully before they are used in research. The following questions will help you determine whether your source is a good one.

Keep in mind that critical reading is the essential skill in evaluating the sources you use. You can learn more about reading critically on page 24.

### Who Wrote It?

Anonymous sources are suspicious—when authors don't attach their names to their assertions, there may be a reason, such as faulty evidence. If the author's name is present, what other information is provided? Look for evidence that might suggest bias—affiliation with an advocacy group or political party, for example. Try to identify the author's purpose and intended audience, and use these to evaluate the potential objectivity of the source. If the topic is controversial, look closely for evidence of bias.

### Where Was It Published?

If the article you are reading was posted on an online forum by *fizz-wizikins*, it is probably not a reliable authority. If it was published by *Oxford University Press*, it probably is. For online sources, check the domain name. The domain *.com* indicates a private or commercial website; *.gov* indicates a government website; *.org* indicates a non-commercial organization. Universities and colleges in Canada all end in *.ca*, but so do many other websites.

## When Was It Published?

Even credible sources can be out of date. Compare recently published data with older data where possible. However, if you are writing a history paper, it might be best to look at information published at the time as well as more recent interpretations of that information. If you are using an Internet source, check to see when the page was last updated. You may be surprised!

## Is the Evidence Used Logical?

People can speculate about and claim all sorts of things, such as "Canada is a bilingual country, so most Canadians are bilingual." Look at the sections in this guide on critical reading (page 24) and the logic of arguments (page 90) before you read sources; they may help you evaluate whether what you read is trustworthy. Be skeptical of claims made without supporting evidence or based on assumptions.

## What Sort of Evidence Is Used?

Has the author of the piece backed up any claims with quotes, statistics, or other evidence? Where did the quotes, statistics, and evidence come from? If information is published by a known reliable source, such as a university or research centre, it is probably reliable. If a source quotes such information, it is probably reliable.

## How Is the Evidence Used?

It is possible to take any piece of information and portray it, out of context, as something it is not. Sources that do this are not credible. Take, for example, the statement "Cherry pickers wash their hands ninety percent of the time when they know they are being filmed, but only fifteen percent of those surveyed said they wash their hands every time they use the washroom." If the author of the piece you are reading stated, "Cherry pickers are the most meticulous of fruit pickers; according to research they wash their hands ninety percent of the time," the information from the original source has been misused. It is a good idea to check original sources where you can.

# Using Sources

## UNDERSTANDING ACADEMIC INTEGRITY

In much of your academic writing, you will be drawing on the ideas and research of others—what in the academic world are called **sources**. You incorporate these ideas into your own writing through quotations, paraphrases, and summaries and identify the source of each idea. The information helps the reader understand the basis for your argument and backs up your assertions. Think of it as a paper trail or a list of obvious clues: you are telling the reader how your thinking developed based on what you researched. If the reader would like to know more about a particular argument or fact that you include in your paper, the information about where that argument or fact came from is right there in your paper in the in-text citations and list of references.

By identifying your sources, you also give credit to the people whose ideas you've used. This practice of acknowledging the sources of the ideas we use in academic writing is an important aspect of what is called **academic integrity**, the expectation that academic writers act honestly and with integrity in their thinking and writing. If you don't acknowledge your sources, you are, whether inadvertently or not, stealing other people's ideas. This is called **plagiarism**. Just as stealing other people's things is considered wrong, so is stealing their intellectual property: their ideas, words, research findings, theories, graphics, designs, and other creations of the mind.

Most universities publish their policy on academic integrity in the academic calendar or elsewhere. If you are a UVic student, refer to the UVic website on academic integrity. It contains information about your rights and responsibilities as a writer. Even though your student life is very busy, take the time to read through this website. It is far easier to avoid a charge of plagiarism than it is to defend yourself against one.

You can violate the principles of academic integrity in a number of ways:

- by submitting someone else's work as your own
- by submitting the same work more than once
- by falsifying research material (making up lab data or misquoting an author)
- by cheating on assignments, tests, or exams
- by failing to give credit to someone else when you use their work
- by helping anyone else to do any of these things

When you do any of these things, you are committing a major form of academic misconduct. If you are caught, you will be penalized and may even be expelled, and the academic community will flag you as a dishonest scholar.

Many instances of academic dishonesty are not intentional. But when it comes to academic writing—writing that is often based on the ideas and words of others—it's necessary to be aware of the dangers of plagiarism, whether accidental and unintentional or a deliberate choice.

## Avoiding Plagiarism

To avoid plagiarism, you must document *all* of your sources. To do this, you must cite every reference to a source, whether a quote, a statistic, or an idea. Every faculty has a preferred documentation style, which you will be expected to use. You can find information on the documentation styles (APA, CMS, CSE, MLA, and IEEE) used by most Canadian universities at the end of this chapter.

Keep careful track of the source of every piece of information you use so that you can be sure to cite it correctly. It is very time consuming to search for the source of a quotation when you aren't sure where it came from; it takes less time to carefully note the source as you plan your writing. See the suggestions in "Keeping Track of Sources" on page 25.

If you are unsure about whether you might be plagiarizing, or if you are worried that you could be, talk to your instructor or TA. Here are some general suggestions concerning the use of source material:

- Always double-check the accuracy of quotations and citations.
- If you alter a quotation, use square brackets [ ] to indicate the change. Be aware, however, that making too many changes can make the quotation sound awkward. If you have to make more than a couple of adjustments, think about paraphrasing.
- Be sure to cite ideas and statistics, even if you have put them into your own words, as well as direct quotations.
- Whenever possible, refer to the original source of material that is quoted within another source.
- Cite each source both in your text and in your list of references.
- If you aren't sure whether something should be cited or not, cite it.

Plagiarism can be a scary topic. Sometimes it seems that to mention it is to suggest that you are considering cheating. If you are uncomfortable talking about plagiarism with your instructor or your TA, talk to a tutor at the writing centre or a learning specialist, such as a librarian.

If you are accused of plagiarism, contact your university's ombudsperson for guidance in navigating the university rules and regulations.

## QUOTING, PARAPHRASING, AND SUMMARIZING

You can incorporate the ideas of others into your academic writing in three ways: by quoting, paraphrasing, and summarizing.

## Quoting

When you quote from a source, you literally put someone else's exact words into your own work. You let your readers know that the words you are using are someone else's and not your own by enclosing the words in quotation marks ("like this"). Quotation marks indicate where a direct quotation begins and ends. You must also acknowledge the source of the quotation by including an appropriate citation or reference at the end of the quote and by including the source in your list of references.

## When to Quote

It's a good idea to quote a passage from a source if

- you are going to discuss, analyze, or critique the exact language of the passage
- its original wording is particularly significant or memorable

If you are primarily interested in the ideas presented in the passage, not its language, it is usually better to paraphrase or summarize.

## How to Quote Effectively

Use the following guidelines to improve your use of quotations.

### Quote only what you need

The purpose of quotations is not to pad your essay; it is to provide relevant support for your argument. Any passage you quote should add helpful information or an insightful point, perhaps providing an example of a concept or principle you have presented. As well, its language should be relevant in some way to the point you are trying to make, either because you will discuss the original wording or because that wording is somehow remarkable. If you can't explain why a quote is in your paper, it shouldn't be there.

Literary essays often discuss the exact language of a text, so quotations might make up as much as thirty percent of these types of papers. In other disciplines, especially those that are less concerned with the specific words used to communicate an idea, quotations should not account for more than ten percent of an essay, and paraphrases or summaries are often preferred.

### Introduce and explain quotations

Since quotations are meant to serve as support for your own points, you should let readers know how to understand and interpret this evidence. A quote that has not been introduced or explained cannot benefit your argument. Therefore, you should not put a quote in your paper without introducing it. It is more helpful still to incorporate it into a sentence and then to discuss or engage with it. Notice how this example uses a quotation effectively:

> In his journal, Private Sullivan states, "Captain Smock was disorganized and illiterate: rather than listening to what the men said about the state of the battle, he simply sent more to the Front" (12). Sullivan's statement shows how the practice of appointing people to high-ranking army positions based on lineage rather than merit caused unnecessary death and prolonged battles.

The quote is introduced in a way that hints at the context in which it first appeared. The sentence that follows the quote explains why it is important, explicitly telling readers what they should take away from this piece of evidence.

### Integrate quotations

Make sure you incorporate quotations into your sentences and paragraphs in a manner that fits grammatically and stylistically. The ideal quotation should fit seamlessly into your work. Incorporation of another writer's words into your text takes time and effort, which is why you might find it easier to paraphrase if you are mainly interested in a passage's ideas, not its wording. To integrate quotations successfully into your own prose, keep the following points in mind.

**Integrating short sections of a prose text:** Short prose quotations should be integrated into your own sentence and paragraph. They are denoted by double quotation marks and should not interrupt the flow of your text.

*Part of a sentence:* Lisa Surridge has suggested that the societal changes brought about by the Industrial Revolution caused "adjustments of class and gender relations across … English society" ("Working-Class" 331).

*A complete sentence:* Gaskell's focus on the role of the father as a parent rather than just a source of finances indicates a shift in the conception of ideal fatherhood: "Gaskell suggests strongly that the emotional poverty of middle-class families arises from their absent fathers" (Surridge 338).

**Integrating long sections of a prose text:** A long prose quotation, one that is at least four lines long (or roughly forty words), should be set off as a block quotation. As with short quotations, it is important to introduce block quotations. Usually, this introduction is handled by a sentence that ends with a colon. The sentences before and after a long quote should discuss the quotation or draw on it for support. A good guideline to remember is that the discussion of a quote should be at least as long as the quote itself. (If you don't have much to say about the quoted passage, it probably shouldn't be in your essay.)

Long quotations are called block quotations because they are set off from regular paragraphs both literally and visually as a block of text: the entire quotation begins on a new line, the entire quotation is indented on both sides, and a new line starts after the quote ends. Quotation marks are unnecessary because the special formatting lets readers know you are quoting.

Example:

> Later, Nick Carroway expresses his frustration with the Buchanans:
>
> > They were careless people, Tom and Daisy—they smashed up things and creatures and retreated back into their money or their vast carelessness, or whatever it was that kept them together, and let other people clean up the mess they had made. (Fitzgerald 114)

**Integrating verse quotations.** Because the most important units of meaning in poetry are groups of lines, not paragraphs or pages, you need to offer readers information about line breaks when you quote verse texts.

*Quoting a short section of verse:* A short quotation of verse is three or fewer lines in length. A quotation that spans more than one line should retain the punctuation and capitalization of the original text and should denote line breaks with a slash (/), leaving a space on either side of the slash.

Example:

> The shift from self-depreciation is sudden; the speaker goes from "curs[ing his] fate" to feeling that his lover's "sweet love such wealth brings / That then [he] scorn[s] to change [his] state with kings" (82).

*Quoting a long section of verse.* Quotations of verse longer than three lines should be treated much like block quotations of prose. They are similarly set off from the regular text, but they also retain the exact lineation, line indentation, and formatting of the original. (If you omit an entire line or more, replace the missing text with a row of spaced periods.)

Example:

> George Herbert's poem "Easter Wings" invokes a pattern of rising and falling both through the pattern of imagery and through the visual structure of the verse on the page:
>
> > Lord, who createdst man in wealth and store,
> >
> > Though foolishly he lost the same,
> >
> > Decaying more and more
> >
> > Till he became
> >
> > Most poor
> >
> > . . . . . .
> >
> > O let me rise
> >
> > . . . . . . . . . . . . . . . . . . . .
> >
> > And sing this day thy victories
> >
> > Then shall the fall further the flight in me. (1026)

### Adapt and alter quotations

**Ensure your tenses agree:** Your paragraph will read smoothly only if the verb tense of your paragraph and your quotation agree. If necessary, you can change the tense of the quotation to fit with your text by using square brackets to indicate your alterations.

| | |
|---|---|
| Original | While the legislators cringe at the sudden darkness, "all eyes were turned to Abraham Davenport." |
| Revised | While the legislators cringe at the sudden darkness, "all eyes [turn] to Abraham Davenport." |

**Ensure your subject and verb agree:** When including a short quotation within a sentence, make sure that the grammatical subject and verb of the sentence agree. You can change the number of the subject or verb contained within the quote so that it fits with the rest of your sentence as long as you put square brackets around the change. Or you can change your wording to better suit the quote.

| | |
|---|---|
| Original | Bell argues that men in the Victorian age "is uptight but well-dressed." (*Men* is the plural form of *man*, so it needs to be followed by *are*.) |
| Revised (1) | Bell argues that men in the Victorian age "[are] uptight but well-dressed." |
| Revised (2) | Bell argues that the average Victorian male "is uptight but well-dressed." |

Provide necessary context

Often, quotations plucked from a longer passage lack contextual information; for example, a pronoun like "it" that once had a clear referent might seem confusing when the sentence in which it appears is removed from a paragraph. You can replace such necessary, important, or clarifying information with words or short phrases in square brackets. Keep in mind, though, that a quote packed with such insertions can be awkward; if you need to add lots of information to make a quotation comprehensible, it would be better to paraphrase.

| | |
|---|---|
| Unclear | "The battle ended in a complete victory." |
| Clarified | "The battle [of Waterloo] ended in a complete victory" for the Alliance. |

Punctuate quotations correctly

The final punctuation of a quotation should be your punctuation, not necessarily that of the original passage. You can usually begin a quotation in the middle of a sentence or eliminate end punctuation silently.

| | |
|---|---|
| Original | "The British Columbian implicit in such displays is beginning to look distressingly stable and discouragingly material" (Dean 59). |
| In the essay | Dean describes the displays as "distressingly stable and discouragingly material" (59), but they continue to draw thousands of tourists. |

However, if you need to change text within a quoted passage, you must mark your alterations. An ellipsis (…) signifies that you have left out words, and square brackets ([]) show that you have changed words.

| | |
|---|---|
| Original | "This last Parliament I called, not more than by others' advice and necessity of my affairs than by my own choice and inclination, who have always thought the right way of Parliaments most safe for my crown and best pleasing to my people." |
| In the essay | Eikon Basilike opens with King Charles I taking responsibility for convening the "last Parliament [that condemned him for treason] … by my own choice and inclination" (3). |

Note that such changes must not alter the meaning of the original text. Misrepresenting what another writer has said, whether intentionally or accidentally, is an improper use of your sources.

## Questions to Consider When Quoting

- Is it important that I use the author's words, or should I paraphrase?
- Is the quotation an appropriate length for my essay?
- Should the quotation be set off as a block quotation?
- Where did I find this? Have I cited it?
- Is my in-text citation correctly formatted?
- Have I indicated any changes I made to the quotation using brackets ([ ]) and ellipses (…)?

# Paraphrasing

When you paraphrase, you rephrase someone else's idea in your own words. Paraphrased ideas must be attributed to the original author by including an appropriate citation or reference at the end of the paraphrase. An introductory phrase or other textual clue should make clear to readers where your own ideas stop and those you are paraphrasing begin.

## When to Paraphrase

Paraphrasing is appropriate when

- you are more interested in conveying an idea presented by a source than in how it is worded
- you can clarify, condense, or streamline the way an idea has been expressed by its author
- you think the original language of the passage is not in keeping with the style or tone of your writing

Unless you have a compelling reason to quote directly, you will find it is often more effective to paraphrase a passage. Paraphrasing gives you greater control over how you incorporate an idea into your written work.

## How to Paraphrase Effectively

Use the following guidelines to improve your use of paraphrases.

### Present the main idea of the original text

The purpose of a paraphrase is to present ideas that appear in a source within the context of your own work. To paraphrase accurately, you need to be sure that you understand and can accurately explain what your source text is saying. It is important, therefore, to look at the passage you want to paraphrase in the context of the larger text. You should be confident about what every word and phrase in the passage means and how it fits into the context of the entire text. Only when you are sure you know what a passage is trying to communicate can you begin to replicate its meaning.

Like a quotation, a paraphrase serves as support for your argument. Unlike a quotation, a paraphrase can often express the idea taken from a source in ways that will be more effective and efficient in the context of your work. For instance, you can condense the original text when you paraphrase, thus leaving yourself more room for analysis and explanation. You can eliminate wordy and confusing phrases, replacing them with your own simple, clear prose. You can even change the order in which an idea was first expressed to make it fit better with your main points.

While you can't change the meaning of a passage when you paraphrase, you can (and should) alter its word choices, syntax, and organization. Such changes should result in a piece of supporting evidence that fits seamlessly into your essay.

### Put the idea in your own words

Paraphrasing, by definition, requires you to put the key point presented in an original text in your own words. Note that if you make only a few minor changes (such as altering verb tenses or skipping a few words) you are actually quoting, and the passage taken from your source should be put in quotation marks with your omissions and additions punctuated appropriately. If you make insufficient changes and offer a paraphrase that too closely replicates a passage's wording or syntax, you are, in effect, plagiarizing by failing to give the original author credit for his or her phrasing.

In the following examples, notice the difference between the "too-close" paraphrase and an appropriate paraphrase from John Locke's *Second Treatise on Government*.

| | |
|---|---|
| Original text | Though the earth, and all inferior creatures, be common to all men, yet every man has a property in his own person: this no body has any right to but himself. The labour of his body, and the work of his hands, we may say, are properly his. Whatsoever then he removes out of the state that nature hath provided, and left it in, he hath mixed his labour with, and joined to it something that is his own, and thereby makes it his property. |
| Too-close paraphrase | Every man has a property in his own person even though the earth and all inferior creatures are common to all men. The work of a man's body and of his hands are properly his. Therefore, whenever he alters something from the state that nature left it in, he mixes it with his labour and thus joins to it something that is his own and thereby makes it his property (Locke 27). |
| Paraphrase | John Locke's theory of property suggests that although the earth and all the creatures on it are owned by all men, whatever a man takes or makes from the earth is his solely because a man's body, and thus the work he produces by using his body, is his alone (27). |

### Introduce and explain paraphrases

Paraphrases derive the ideas they present from another person's work, so they need to end by giving credit to the source of the ideas. A paraphrase always ends either with a parenthetical citation or some other kind of reference depending on the style guide being followed. It should be easy, therefore, for readers to tell when your paraphrase stops and your own ideas begin.

But how can readers tell when you are shifting from your points to the beginning of a paraphrase? Unlike a quotation, a paraphrase doesn't signal its start with quotation marks. To help your readers tell which ideas are yours and which are derived from a source, make it clear when you are beginning to present evidence based on another author's work.

The typical way to indicate the start of a paraphrase is with an opening signal phrase. Such phrases offer you an opportunity to give readers basic contextual information about the paraphrase they are about to encounter.

| | |
|---|---|
| Sample signal phrases | Stephen Greenblatt's analysis of Hamlet points out that … |
| | David Suzuki has argued that … |
| | A recent *Globe and Mail* editorial explains that … |
| | The latest study by climate scientists revealed … |
| | Henderson says … |

Sometimes you might want to work a signal phrase into a more complex introduction to a paraphrase that explains what readers should derive from this particular piece of evidence.

Sample introductions    Stephen Harper's speech surprised many pundits by presenting as its key point …

The newspaper editorial will not persuade most university
students because it omits any consideration of costs while
declaring we should be most concerned about …

In either case, you should make it as easy for readers to distinguish between para-
phrased material and your original text as it is to see the difference between text inside and outside of quotation marks.

## Summarizing

When you summarize, you rephrase a section of a longer piece of writing, an entire work, or even a whole book in a short space, often no more than a few sentences. Although you are using your own words when you summarize, you must attribute the source of the ideas. Summaries usually start with a phrase that provides necessary context, and they always end with an appropriate citation or reference that acknowledges the original author.

### When to Summarize

It is best to summarize when

- the main idea of a long passage, not its details or expression, is key to the point you want to make

- you need to present the ideas of another writer (or many other writers) concisely so that you can emphasize your own analysis, critique, or argument

### How to Summarize Effectively

For a detailed discussion of how to summarize, including guidance on how to write an effective summary, see "Writing a Research Paper" on page 101.

## DOCUMENTATION STYLES

When you quote, paraphrase, or summarize someone else's idea, you must acknowledge the author and provide details of the source in two ways:

- within your text, immediately following the quotation, paraphrase, or use of someone else's idea; these are called **in-text citations**

- at the end of your paper, in the form of a **bibliography**, a **works cited** list, or a **references** list, depending on the style you are using

Below you will find a summary of the documentation preferences of each of the five most popular academic writing styles used in North America:

- APA style
- CMS style

- CSE style
- IEEE style
- MLA style

The examples and guidelines below cover only the sources most commonly used in student papers. If you do not find an example for the type of source you are using, look for style guides at your university library website or search online for style guidelines. The University of Victoria libraries publish citation guides for all the major styles and provide online access to the *Chicago Manual of Style*.

If you expect to use a style regularly in your academic work, it is a good idea to buy a copy of the latest version of the style guide, which will cover all possible sources, including new media, as well as formatting guidelines and editiorial style guidelines. If you have your own copy, you can flag or highlight the sections you most often use.

## APA (American Psychological Association)

APA style is widely used in the social sciences as well as in education, nursing, social work, public administration, and many other disciplines.

The following guidelines cover in-text citations and reference citations for only the most commonly used sources. For more detailed information, or for examples of sources not listed here, refer to the *Publication Manual of the American Psychological Association* (6th ed.).

### APA In-text Citations

APA uses author-date style: the author of a source and the date it was published are indicated in parentheses immediately following a quotation, idea, paraphrase, or summary from that source. The author's name and the publication date are separated by a comma.

Example          Doctors caution that switching to a sugar-free diet is not a cure for epilepsy (Higgs, 2003).

If the author's name appears in the sentence, place the year in parentheses immediately after the name. If the author and date have already appeared in a paragraph, do not repeat the author and date within the same paragraph.

Example          Schoen (2001) then argued that there were many different ways to lower the number of seizures experienced by epileptics (p. 5). He stated that changes in diet could not change the number of seizures experienced by epileptics (pp. 12–14).

Include a page reference if you quote the author or cite a specific piece of information.

Example          The study concluded that a sugar-free diet "is not a cure for epilepsy" (Higgs, 2003, p. 23).

### Work by one author

If you are citing a work by one author, place the name of the author and the date of the work in parentheses, separated by a comma.

Example          (Burns, 1999)

### Work by two to five authors

If you are citing a source that has up to five authors, give all names the first time you mention them, either within the text of your essay or in parentheses. In parentheses, use an ampersand (&) instead of *and*.

Example                Williams, Mehta, and Morris (2003) argue …
                                (Williams, Mehta, & Clark, 2003)

### Subsequent citations

Subsequent citations of a work by one or two authors follow the same rules as for the first citation. In the case of a work by three or more authors, give the first author's name followed by *et al.*

Example                Williams et al. (2003) argue …

### Organization as author

If citing an organization, write out the full name of the organization in your first in-text citation and include an abbreviation in brackets; use the abbreviation thereafter.

Example                first citation: (The Federal Bureau of Investigation [FBI], 2001)
                                subsequent citations: (FBI, 2001)

### Unknown author

If the author of a work is unknown, cite the work by its title.

Example                ("Epilepsy and Food," 2003, p. 14)

### Authors with the same name

If you are citing works by authors with the same last name, include their initial(s) in the citations.

Example                (K. Jones, 2002)
                                (H. G. Jones, 2008)

### More than one work by an author

If you are quoting more than one work by the same author, list all dates.

Example                (Schoen, 1998, 2001, 2004)

If you are listing two or more works written by the same author in the same year, label the dates with letters.

Example                (Schoen, 1998a)
                                (Schoen, 1998b)

### Two or more works in one citation

If you are citing more than one work in a sentence or passage, include all the works in one set of parentheses, separated by semicolons. Cite the authors in alphabetical order.

Example                (Burns, 1999; Morris, 2003; Schoen, 1998c)

### Undated work

If the publication date is unknown, use *n.d.*

Example                (Cassey, n.d.)

Unpaginated online material

If you are citing an online source that does not provide page numbers, give paragraph numbers, if provided, and use the abbreviation *para*.

Example                    (Xiao, 2003, para. 12)

If the source does not include either page numbers or paragraph numbers, give the heading under which the cited material appears and the number of the paragraph following the heading.

Example                    (Results section, para. 3)

APA References

All works that are cited in the text are referenced in a list, entitled *References*, that appears at the end of your paper. The general rules for this list are as follows:

* List each work alphabetically by the author's last name or by title if the author is unknown.
* Give the author's last name and initials only, and leave a space between the author's initials.
* If an author has more than one work, place the works in chronological order, by the year in which they were published.
* Use a hanging indention of 0.5" for any references of more than one line.
* Capitalize only the first word, any proper nouns, and the first word following a colon in titles of books and journal articles.
* Capitalize all major words in journal titles.
* Italicize the titles of books and journals (including the volume number but not the issue number).
* Do not italicize the titles of journal articles or enclose them in quotation marks.
* Include the publication city and publisher for books. Include both the city and the state, province, or country in all references.
* Use the ampersand (&) instead of *and* with more than one name.
* Do not include a URL for online sources with DOIs (digital object identifiers).

| APA References | |
|---|---|
| **Type of Citation** | **Example** |
| Book by one author | Hake, S. (2002). *German national cinema*. New York, NY: Routledge. |
| Book by two or more authors | Choi, P. S., Kim, J. K., & Simkins, D. (2005). *Self esteem in children*. New York, NY: Routledge. |
| Book with editor | Swisher, C. (Ed.). (2000). *Victorian England*. San Diego, CA: Greenhaven Press. |
| Book with editors | Dickson, F. A., & Smythe, S. (Eds.). (1970). *The Writer's Digest handbook of short story writing*. Cincinnati, OH: Writer's Digest Books. |

| Chapter in a book | Pasque, C. B. (2009). Women in combat sports. In A. W. Wallace, R. R. Wroble, N. Maffulli, & R. Kordi (Eds.), *Combat sports medicine* (pp. 1-15). London, UK: Springer. |
|---|---|
| Review | Bashford, L. (2001, March). [Review of the book *The Good Body*, by Bill Gaston]. *Malahat Review, 134*, 111–113. |
| Article from a print journal | Jackson, M. R. (2011). Psychology and social justice. *Peace Review, 23*(1), 69-76.<br>Note: If no page numbers are available, the reference should end *Volume*(Issue). |
| Article from an online journal—no DOI | Cunningham, J. A., Kypri, K., & McCambridge, J. (2011). The use of emerging technologies in alcohol treatment. *Alcohol Research and Health, 33*(4). Retrieved from http://pubs.niaaa.nih.gov/publications/arh334/320-326.htm |
| Article from an online journal—with DOI | Zagury, F. (2009). Sidelight on the diffuse interstellar bands problem. *Open Astronomy Journal, 2*, 58–62. doi: 10.2174/1874381100902010058 |
| Technical report | Ford, J. K., Koot, B., Vagle, S., Hall-Patch, N., & G. Kamitakahara. (2010). *Passive acoustic monitoring of large whales in offshore waters of British Columbia* (Technical Report 2898). Retrieved from Fisheries and Oceans Canada website: http://www.dfo-mpo.gc.ca/libraries-bibliotheques/tech-eng.htm |
| Online magazine article | Cosh, C. (2010, October 9). Meet your kids' new roommate: The bedbug. *Maclean's*. Retrieved from http://www2.macleans.ca/2010/10/09/new-roommate-the-bedbug/ |
| Online newspaper article | Moses, A. (2006, December 14). Wii breaks Xbox 360 sales record. *Sydney Morning Herald*. Retrieved from http://www.smh.com.au/News/article/3060 |
| Web page | Bell, M. (2010). *Cocoa: benefits and myths*. Retrieved from http://chocoa.com<br>Note: Do not include retrieval date unless the content is likely to change over time. |

## CMS (Chicago Manual of Style)

Chicago style is used in many disciplines, including humanities and business. Chicago style allows for both author-date and note systems for in-text citations. Only the note system is described below. For details on how to use the author-date system, refer to the *Chicago Manual of Style*.

### CMS In-Text Citations and Notes

There are several variations in Chicago style, but Chicago recommends that you use short footnote entries that correspond to superscript numbers in your text and a bibliography at the end of your paper. If you choose not to include a bibliography, your footnotes will have to include all the bibliographic information.

### Where to place numbers

Superscript numbers are placed after a quoted word or phrase or at the end of a sentence, following the end punctuation.

Example                          GGT stock fell 30 percent in the first quarter.[3]

Each in-text superscript must be accompanied by a footnote that begins with the corresponding number in the text.

Full bibliographic details are provided the first time a source is cited. Note that the citation begins with the author's first name. The first line is indented five spaces.

Example                          3. Peter A. Baskerville, *Ontario: Image, Identity, and Power*. Don Mills, ON: Oxford University Press, 2002.

Subsequent citations require only a shortened version of the same citation.

Example                          3. Baskerville, *Ontario,* 34.

### Citing multiple sources in one place

If you are citing more than one source in the same location, use a single superscript number and list all sources under the same number. Use a semicolon to separate the works within the note.

Example                          GGT stock rose to overtake HFG stock by the end of the fiscal year.[4]
                                 4. GGT, "Company Review 2002," 12; Hendrix, "Surprises of 2002," 45.

### Citing one source consecutively

If the same source is used in consecutive notes, use the notation *Ibid.* to indicate that the source is the same as the previous one.

Example                          Ontario is often seen as more powerful than other provinces,3 but this image has changed recently due to a recent diversification of trading partners.4
                                 3. Baskerville, *Ontario*, 35.
                                 4. Ibid., 68–71.

### Works by multiple authors

To cite a work by two or three authors, include all of the authors' names.

Example                          18. Piper and Jones, *History of Unemployment,* 98.
                                 18. Piper, Jones, and Haast, *History of Unemployment,* 98.

To cite a work with more than three authors, write *et al* or *and others*.

Example                          18. Piper et al., *History of Unemployment,* 98–102.
                                 18. Piper and others, *History of Unemployment,* 98–102.

### Works by unknown authors

If an author in unknown, list the work under its title.

Example                          13. *History of Unemployment,* 98–102.

### Work with editor

If a work is listed under its editor, begin the note with the editor's name instead of the author's. You do not need to indicate within the note that the work is listed under its editor's name; the bibliographic entry will show this.

| | |
|---|---|
| Note | 13. Piper, *History of Unemployment,* 98–102. |
| Bibliographic Entry | Piper, Peter P., ed. *History of Unemployment.* London: Swotty Press, 2000. |

### CMS Bibliography

CMS style calls for a full bibliography when shortened footnotes are used. It should be titled *Bibliography*.

If you have used full footnotes, you do not need to include a bibliography, although many journals and instructors ask for both.

The use of a bibliography and shortened footnotes is recommended for clarity and ease of use. If you have used this style of citation, your footnotes will correspond with a list at the end of your essay that includes all the works you have referenced. The general rules for this list are as follows:

- List each work alphabetically by the author's last name.
- Use a hanging indention for entries of more than one line.
- Capitalize all major words in titles and the first word following a colon.

For more information or to see examples for sources not included here, please refer to the *Chicago Manual of Style* or your university library's website.

## CMS Bibliography

| Type of Citation | Example |
|---|---|
| Book by one author | Hake, Sabine. *German National Cinema.* New York: Routledge, 2002. |
| Book by two or more authors | Cobin, Harold, Chris Shutter, and Mary Lawson. *Novels and Novellas: A History.* New York: NY Books, 2002. |
| Book by a corporate author | David Suzuki Foundation. *On Thin Ice: Winter Sports and Climate Change.* Vancouver: David Suzuki Foundation, 2009. |
| Book with editor/translator | Swisher, Clarice, ed. *Victorian England.* San Diego: Greenhaven Press, 2000. If the book has multiple editors, use *eds.* in place of *ed.* If it has a translator, use *trans.* |
| Book with editor/translator and author | Blais, Marie-Claire. *Thunder and Light.* Translated by Nigel Spencer. Anansi: Don Mills, 2001. |
| Part of an anthology, collection, or multiauthor book | Faulkner, William. "That Evening Sun Go Down." In *The Best American Short Stories of the Century*, eds. John Updike and Katrina Kenison, 111–26. New York: Houghton Mifflin, 2000. |

| Article from a print journal | Kelly, Gavin. "Ammianus and the Great Tsunami." *Journal of Roman Studies* 94, no. 141 (2004): 141–67. |
|---|---|
| Article from an online journal or database | Reference an online journal article as you would a print article, but add a URL or a DOI to the end of the citation. |
| | Kelly, Gavin. "Ammianus and the Great Tsunami." *Journal of Roman Studies* 94, no. 141 (2004): 141-67. doi:10.1353/jla.0.0029. |
| | Kelly, Gavin. "Ammianus and the Great Tsunami." *Journal of Roman Studies* 94, no. 141 (2004): 141-67. http://www.jstor.org.ezproxy.library.uvic.ca/stable/4135013 |
| Online newspaper article | Moses, Asher. "Wii Breaks Xbox 360 Sales Record." *Sydney Morning Herald*, December 14, 2006. http://www.smh.com.au/news/games/wii-breaks-xbox-sales-record/2006/12/14/1165685799546.html. |
| Website | Include a publication date or date of latest revision or, if no publication date is available, include an access date. |
| | Bell, Madeline. "Cocoa: Benefits and Myths." http://chocoa.com (accessed June 17, 2009). |

# CSE (Council of Science Editors)

CSE style is often used for scientific writing. It has three approved types of in-text citation; however, the citation-sequence system (detailed below) is the simplest.

## CSE In-text Citations

### Where to place numbers

The citation-sequence system uses superscripted numbers that refer to a list of references at the end of the work. The numbers are placed within the text, before the punctuation at the end of a clause or phrase.

If you are citing two sources, separate their numbers with a comma and a space (4, 5). If you are referencing three or more references, separate their numbers with an en-dash (3–5).

CSE style calls for a space before the superscripted number. Leave a space after the superscripted number if it is followed by text (Jenkins [5] states that) but not if it is followed by punctuation (as stated by Higgins [7], author of *T Cells*).

Example

Schoen has suggested that CSE style is used widely by science writers [4,5]; the Council of Science Editors agrees [6]. They have released a book detailing how to write in CSE style, which complies with the standards set out in their five online publications [7-12].

### Using parenthetical numbers

Some CSE publications call for these numbers to be written within parentheses instead of superscripted.

| Example | Schoen (4, 5) has suggested that CSE style is used widely by science writers; the Council of Science Editors (6) agrees. They have released a book detailing how to write in CSE style. |

Check to see whether your instructor prefers parenthetical or superscripted citations.

### Number sequencing

Numbers occur in sequence, whether they are superscripted or parenthetical. References appear in the reference list in the same sequence—not alphabetically—and are labelled by citation number.

| Citation | Schoen (4) has suggested that ... |
| Bibliographic Entry | 4. Schoen JH. Using CSE style: the basics. New York: Science Publishing House; 1997. p. 789. |

## CSE Cited References

CSE style allows for several types of bibliographic list, called either *References* or *Cited References*. The simplest, which corresponds with the citation-sequence system, is outlined below. The general rules for this list are as follows:

- List works numerically, in the sequence in which you cited them.
- List authors by last name followed by initials, with no comma between the last name and the initials, no period after initials, and no space between initials.
- In titles, capitalize only the first word and proper nouns, and do not italicize.

For more information or to see examples of sources not included here, consult *Scientific Style and Format: The CSE Manual for Authors, Editors, and Publishers, 7th ed.*

| **CSE Cited References** | |
| --- | --- |
| **Type of Citation** | **Example** |
| Book with one author | 1. Smith JK. Medications for cows. 4th ed. Toronto (ON): Veterinary Guides Inc.; 2002. |
| Book with two or more authors | 2. Higgins ML, Pritt J. Herpes simplex: heat and infection rate. New York (NY): Scientific Press; 2000. |
| Part of an edited book | 3. Jigs, M. Interplanetary forces. In: Swisher C, editor. Astrophysics. San Diego (CA): Greenhaven; 2000. p.121–129. |
| Book with editor(s), no author | 4. Dickson FA, Smythe S, editors. The Writer's Digest handbook of short story writing. Cincinnati (OH): Writer's Digest Books; 1970. |
| Article from a print journal | 5. Amedi J, Liu K. Supernovas and the truth quark. J Asphys Quart. 2002; 78(3):34–43. |

| Article from an online journal or database | Reference an online journal article as you would a print article, but include the URL and access date. Include the medium in brackets after the title. |
|---|---|
| | 6. Slisky B. Abnormalities in sickle-celled anemia. Blood [Internet]. 2009 [cited 2010 Jan 27]; 21(1):8–13. Available from: http://places.designobserver.com/media/pdf/Adventures_in__940.pdf. |
| Conference papers | 8. Gibby J. Swine flu: permutations of flu. WHO conference; 2009 Dec 12–15; Vancouver, BC. Vancouver (BC): University of British Columbia; 2010. p. 12–21. |
| Technical reports | 9. Potter H. Minions of the dark side. London (UK): Magical Publications Inc.; 2001. Report No. TR89485. |
| Other reports | 10. Ganing J. Lymphoma in mice treated with antiretrovirals. Report. Cambridge (UK): CancerMice; 2004. |
| Website | 11. History of chocolate [Internet]. Calgary (AB): Association of Chocolate Lovers; 2003 [cited 2010 June 4]. Available from: http://inventors.about.com/od/foodrelatedinventions/a/chocolate.htm. |

## IEEE (Institute of Electrical and Electronics Engineers)

### In-text Citation

IEEE style has a very simple form of in-text citation: a number set in square brackets that falls before the punctuation at the end of a clause, phrase, or sentence and refers to a numbered list of references at the end of the work.

Example          The bridge was designed with equilateral triangles to increase its strength [1].

These numbers should correspond with the numbers you have given works in your references section. Because your in-text citation numbers correspond with your references list, they will not necessarily proceed in sequence as footnotes would. However, as your references will be listed in the order you have cited them, the numbers will be in sequence unless you cite a single work several times throughout your paper (as in the example below).

Example          Recent studies have found these practices substandard [1], [22].

For more information and to see how to format your reference list, consult the IEEE online style guide.

### IEEE References

Bibliographic entries for works using IEEE style are included at the end of the work in a list titled *References*. The general rules for this list are as follows:

- List works numerically, in the sequence in which you cited them. If you have cited a work more than once in your paper, use the same number for each in-text citation; do not include the work in your references twice.

- Capitalize only the first word and any proper nouns in titles of short works.
- Capitalize all major words in titles of long works.
- List authors by their initials first, followed by their last names. Each initial is followed by a period and a space.
- If a Digital Object Identifier (DOI) is provided, add it in place of page numbers or, if both page numbers and a DOI are provided, add the DOI after the page numbers.
- Abbreviate titles of periodicals and conference proceedings. You can find a list of standard abbreviations used in IEEE citations by searching online.

## IEEE References

| Type of Citation | Example |
| --- | --- |
| Book by one author | [1] T. L. Koglin, *Movable Bridge Engineering*. Hoboken, NJ: J. Wiley & Sons, 2003. |
| Book by two or three authors | [2] J. E. Shigley and C. R. Mischke, *Mechanical Engineering Design,* 5th ed. New York, NY: McGraw-Hill, 1989. |
| Chapter or article in a book | [3] A. Tenshun, "Random oscillations," in *Why Bridges Collapse,* B. Reddy, Ed. Minneapolis, MN: Paper Press, 2001, pp. 55–61. |
| Patents | [4] M. Pathy, "Pain reduction bracelet," U.S. Patent 76 875 808, July 14, 2003. |
| Reports | [5] E. Tapley, "Technical components of motherboards," Heliotrope Computer Co., Toronto, ON, Rep. JH-276-09-767, 2010. |
| Handbooks | [6] *Handbook of Handbooks,* 3rd ed., Handbooks Co., Phoenix, AZ, 1999, pp. 234–267. |
| Standards | [7] *IEEE Criteria for Class IE Electric Systems,* IEEE Standard 308, 1969. |
| Conference papers | [8] M. Ibrahim *et al.,* "Creative design dynamics and creative systems," in *Proc. 2009 IEEE Int. Systems Conf.,* Vancouver, BC, 2003, pp. 273-278. doi: 10.1109/SYSTEMS.2009.4815811 |
| Theses and dissertations | [9] A. Svestrup, "The physics of joints in cantilever bridges," Ph.D. dissertation, Dep. Comp. Eng., Waikato Univ., Hamilton, New Zealand, 1965. |
| Article from a print journal | [10] Z. Xia *et al.,* "Global navigation for humanoid robots using sampling-based footstep planners," *IEEE/ASME Trans. Mechatron,* vol. 16, no. 4, pp. 716-723, Aug. 2011. |
| Article from an online journal | [11] A. Schmidt and D. Bial, "Phones and MP3 players as the core component in future appliances," *IEEE Pervasive Comput.* vol. 10, no. 2, pp. 8-11, Feb. 2011. doi: 10.1109/MPRV.2011.31 |

# MLA (Modern Language Association)

MLA style is most often used in the humanities.

## MLA In-text Citation

To cite in MLA style, place the author's last name and the number of the page referenced within parentheses at the end of the clause or sentence in which you have included a quote or information from a work. If you are referencing an entire work, you can leave out the page number. Place any punctuation after the parenthetical citation.

Example          The wife proclaims that she can no longer "stand to see Mr. Foster treat his daughter in such a manner" (Biggs 143).

## Citing a work repeatedly

If you are citing the same source twice within a sentence (or repeatedly within a paragraph), do not include the author's name in the second citation.

Example          The wife proclaims that she can no longer "stand to see Mr. Foster treat his daughter in such a manner" (Biggs 143), after which she marches into her husband's study and demands that he "behave as fits a gentleman" and intervene (145).

However, if you are citing multiple authors, leave out the author's name only if you are certain that there can be no confusion over which author wrote what.

Example          Mrs. Higgins decides to "assert the power of a matriarch" after seeing the way Mr. Foster treats Millie (Groen 345); she marches into her husband's study and demands that he "behave as fits a gentleman" and intervene (Biggs 145).

## Author mentioned in body of paper

If you mention the name of the author of your source within the sentence in which you are citing, you do not need to include the name in the parenthetical citation.

Example          Biggs empowers women by having Mrs. Higgins march into her husband's study and demand that he "behave as fits a gentleman" and intervene (145). He continues with this theme by having the Fosters' maid, Mary, stand between Millie and her father later in the chapter (157).

## Multiple works by one author

If you are using more than one work by an author, include the title or subtitle of the work in your in-text citation. If you include the name of the author and the name of the work, use a comma between the two names. Do not place a comma between the name of the work and the page number.

Example          Biggs empowers women by having Mrs. Higgins march into her husband's study and demand that he "behave as fits a gentleman" and intervene (*The Trials of Millie Foster* 145). The argument that this is an "assert[ion of] the power of a matriarch" (Biggs, "Mad Mothers" 345) is flawed, however, given the context in which this incident occurs.

Authors with the same name

If you are citing two authors with the same last name, include initials.

Example                    (A. Biggs 45) (F. Biggs 253)

Works by multiple authors

If a work has two or three authors, list all of the authors in the citation.

Example                    (Jones and Huang 56) (Higgins, Burke, and Joyce 245)

If a work has more than three authors, list only one author followed by *et al.*

Example                    (Burkley et al. 56)

Works by an anonymous author

If a work is anonymous, use the title of the work instead of the author's name.

Example                    ("Working in Industry" 127)

Quotes within sources

If you are using a quote from within a work, indicate that the source is indirect.

Example                    (qtd. in Hutch 234)

Poetry, verse, and plays

If you are citing lines of a poem, cite the lines as you would pages.

Example                    (Donne 10–14)

If you are citing the Bible, list the title of the book, the chapter, and the verse or verses. Note that there is no space between the colon and the verse numbers.

Example                    (Isaiah 29:3–15)

If you are citing a play, cite the act, the scene, and the lines (or pages, if no line numbers are given), separated by periods: (*Title* or Author Act.Scene.Lines). The same can be done for long poems that are separated into parts.

Example                    (*Othello* 1.3.12–13) (Miller 2.1.14)

For more information or to see examples of cited works, please refer to the *MLA Handbook for Writers of Research Papers, 7th Edition.*

## MLA Works Cited List

All works that you cite in text are referenced in a list entitled *Works Cited,* which appears at the end of your essay. The general rules for this list are as follows:

- List each work alphabetically by the author's last name.
- Use a 1.25 cm hanging indention for any references of more than one line.
- Italicize titles of books and journals.
- Capitalize all major words in titles.
- Use quotation marks to enclose the titles of articles within works.
- Include the medium of the source cited (e.g., *Print, Web, PDF*).

Below are examples of the works-cited entries for sources commonly cited in MLA papers.

## MLA Works Cited

| Type of Citation | Example |
| --- | --- |
| Book by one author | Hake, Sabine. *German National Cinema*. New York: Routledge, 2002. Print. |
| Book by two or three authors | Campbell, Patricia Shehan, and Carol Scott-Kassner. *Music in Childhood*. Boston: Schirmer, 2006. Print. |
| Book with editor | Swisher, Clarice, ed. *Victorian England*. San Diego: Greenhaven, 2000. Print. |
| Book with editors | Dickson, Frank A., and Sandra Smythe, eds. *The Writer's Digest Handbook of Short Story Writing*. Cincinnati: Writer's Digest Books, 1970. Print. |
| Poem, short story, or poem in an edited anthology | Faulkner, William. "That Evening Sun Go Down." *The Best American Short Stories of the Century*. Ed. John Updike and Katrina Kenison. New York: Houghton Mifflin, 2000. 111–26. Print. |
| Review | Bashford, Lucy. Rev. of *The Good Body*, by Bill Gaston. *Malahat Review* 134 (2001): 111–13. Print. |
| Article from a journal (print) | Kelly, Gavin. "Ammianus and the Great Tsunami." *Journal of Roman Studies* 94 (2004): 141–67. Print. |
| Article from a journal (online) | Sahotsky, Brian. "Adventures in Architectural Symbolism: The Use and Misuse of Rebuilding Programs in Ancient Rome." *Places* 21.1 (2009): 8–13. Web. 27 Jan. 2010. |
| Article from a database | Rentschler, Eric. "Mountains and Modernity: Relocating the Bergfilm." *New German Critique* 51 (1990): 137–61. *Academic Search Premier*. Web. 25 Jan. 2010. |
| Online newspaper article | Moses, Asher. "Wii Breaks Xbox 360 Sales Record." *Sydney Morning Herald* 14 Dec. 2006. Web. 30 Aug. 2007. |
| Online encyclopedia or dictionary entry | "Squiggle." *Oxford English Dictionary*. 6th ed. Oxford: Oxford UP, 1999. Web. 14 Jul. 2009. |
| Website | Bellis, Mary. "The Culture of the Cocoa Bean." *History of Chocolate*. About.com, 16 Sept. 2009. Web. 17 Jun. 2010. |
| Film or video | *Doubt*. Dir. John Patrick Shanley. Perf. Meryl Streep, Philip Seymour Hoffman, and Amy Adams. Miramax, 2008. DVD. |

# Improving Your Writing Skills

The ways to develop your academic writing skills are described throughout the rest of part 1 of this guide—learning to use the academic writing process effectively, becoming an active and critical reader, developing research skills, and mastering the conventions of documentation. All of these will help you succeed as an academic writer.

This section focuses on improving your actual writing—the way you construct paragraphs, the way you craft sentences, and the way you choose words to express your ideas. As you learn to pay attention to your writing—how your words, sentences, and paragraphs communicate your meaning—you will find that academic writing becomes much easier.

## WRITING STRONG PARAGRAPHS

Paragraphs are the building blocks of academic writing, dividing your work into understandable sections that fit together within a unified whole.

Learning to write focused, organized, well-developed paragraphs will improve your writing in two important ways: it will help you control the way you present your ideas, and it will make your meaning easier for your reader to understand.

A well-written paragraph is defined by three characteristics: unity, coherence, and adequate development.

## Unity

Every paragraph you write should have one central idea, which is developed fully within the paragraph. The clear and focused development of this central idea is referred to as **paragraph unity**. In a unified paragraph, every sentence—from the first to the last—works to support and develop the main idea.

### Topic Sentences

The focus of each paragraph is announced in its **topic sentence.** In academic writing, the topic sentence is generally the first sentence of the paragraph, although it may also appear at the end.

Here are some typical topic sentences. Notice how clearly they announce what the paragraph will be about:

> While Canada's current unemployment rate is still lower than it was during the Great Depression, its impact on society is much greater.

> The Australian possum provides yet another example of the devastation that introduced species can wreak on an environment.

> During the winter following the Frog Lake Massacre, the hardships of the Cree people increased.

A common error among inexperienced writers is to compose paragraphs with more than one topic. If you find that a paragraph you have written has two topics, you need to reassess the purpose of the paragraph and alter your topic sentence or give the second idea its own paragraph.

## Supporting Sentences

Each sentence within the paragraph should support—and directly relate to—the topic sentence. If a sentence does not support the topic sentence, it should not be included.

Notice how the sentences in the following paragraph support one main idea, set out in the topic sentence:

> There are two philosophies of medicine: the primitive or superstitious, and the modern or rational. They are in complete opposition to one another. The former involves the belief that disease is caused by supernatural forces. Such a doctrine associates disease with sin; it is an aspect of religion that conceives diseases as due to certain forms of evil and attempts to control them by ceremonial and superstitious measures or to drive them away by wishful thinking. On the other hand, rational medicine is based on the conception that disease arises from natural causes.

If the topic sentence were "Primitive medicine was the primary philosophy of early physicians" but the paragraph then went on to discuss modern medicine, the paragraph would need to be adjusted or split in two.

## Concluding Sentences

Summarizing each paragraph is just as important as defining your topic sentence. The concluding sentence should answer the proverbial question, "So what?" Without it, your readers may be confused about what conclusion you want them to reach. Do not assume they will come to the same conclusion as you; instead, state your conclusion clearly.

| | |
|---|---|
| Topic sentence | The idea that the monsters of horror fiction are embodiments or manipulations of inner, psychic forces is a commonplace in the discourse of the genre. |
| Concluding sentence | But even here [referencing an example] the assumption can be made that the audience will understand and accept that the Alien "is actually the enemy inside us all." |

# Coherence

A paragraph is **coherent** if the ideas within it are arranged in a way that makes sense to the reader. You can achieve coherence by arranging your sentences so that each is connected to the previous one and leads to the next.

The actual arrangement of sentences within a paragraph depends on both the purpose of the paragraph and its position within the essay. For example, an introduction usually moves from general statements to specific facts and claims, while a conclusion usually moves from specific facts from the essay to general statements that place its findings within a wider context.

Use structure to your advantage: a paragraph with a specific direction is more powerful than one that presents information randomly.

Common Paragraph Patterns

In academic writing, there are several common patterns that will give your paragraphs coherence.

**Go from the general to the particular.** The general to particular strategy is particularly effective in an introduction, but can be used elsewhere.

To use the pattern, introduce your topic with a general topic sentence, such as "In Shakespeare's England, a standing army was unknown: there was no general military organization." From here, describe the topic in increasing detail.

**Go from the particular to the general.** The opposite strategy, moving from particular to general, can be just as effective; it is often used in the conclusion to an essay. Note how the following begins with specific dates and actions, and then draws them all together into a general observation:

> Nineteen forty-eight saw the beginning of the systematic suppression of the Greek guerrillas—a rather baffling police operation executed by indigenous forces, with the United States supplying only material aid and technical advice. Nineteen forty-nine was the year that turned the tide in Berlin—through a massive logistic effort carried out primarily by the Americans themselves…. In sum, the containment policy rests on the idea of a strategic reserve—a flexible concept as opposed to the static and impossible notion of simply manning a wall.

**Tell a story (narrate).** The best way to structure a historical or biographical paragraph may simply be to tell a story. In literary essays, however, be careful not to spend unnecessary time recounting the plot for the benefit of an instructor who knows it well.

> In the 1950s, French fries were an unimportant side dish that brought in little profit at most restaurants. The McDonald brothers, however, gave considerable attention to their French fries. Many of their customers were fiercely devoted to the product. Ray Kroc believed the McDonald's fries were the best he had ever tasted. Convinced that they would be crucial to the success of his chain, he set out to master French fry production.

**Follow a chronology.** A chronology explains by listing events in their order through time; it is a particular kind of narrative. The sequence of events is important, and is carefully signalled:

> The new earth, freshly torn from its parent sun, was a ball of whirling gases, intensely hot, rushing through the black spaces of the universe on a path at a speed controlled by immense forces. Gradually the ball of flaming gases cooled. The gases began to liquefy, and Earth became a molten mass.

## Paragraph Development

Each paragraph you write must be developed in enough detail for your reader to understand the point you are making. How much detail is enough depends on the topic and your larger argument, but in academic writing, paragraphs of two or three sentences are not usually fully developed.

Here are several strategies you can use to develop interesting, well-supported, varied paragraphs. These will help you approach your topic from different angles to create a stronger essay.

## Use Examples

Provide specific examples that support your argument. For each example, provide an explanation and link the example to your essay thesis and the paragraph topic.

> In recent years, many former colonies have attempted to redress the wrongs done to indigenous populations at the time of colonization. In British Columbia, for example, extensive redressive treaty negotiations have been ongoing for over a decade; a settlement was recently reached with the Tsawwassen First Nation, which saw their lands increase from 290 hectares to 720 hectares.

## Analyze

Subdivide a topic and analyze each subtopic within your paragraph.

> There are six flavours of quark: up, down, top, bottom, charm, and strange. The up quark and the down quark combine to make up protons and neutrons. The charmed quark and the strange quark are found in hadrons.

## Compare

There are two ways to structure comparisons. You can compare each separate subtopic with its equal and opposite subtopic or you can compare an entire topic with its equal and opposite topic. For example, for two topics (A and B) and three subtopics (1, 2, and 3), your comparison could take either of the following forms:

- paragraph one discusses A1 and B1; paragraph two discusses A2 and B2; and paragraph three discusses A3 and B3
- paragraph one discusses A1, A2, and A3; paragraph two discusses B1, B2, and B3

## Define Terms

Define and explain the significance of key terms.

> A variable cost is directly proportionate to the number of units produced or services given. This means that if a business produces more of a certain product, their overhead will increase proportionately. Fixed costs, on the other hand, remain the same whether or not more units are produced and include salaries, rent, and insurance. If a company's variable costs and fixed costs are less than the amount it makes selling its products or services, it will profit. If, however, the variable and fixed costs add to more than the company makes, it will decline and eventually go bankrupt.

## Explain Causes

Make a claim and then provide the explanation for it.

> The development of advertising styles was the result of the convergence of several very respectable American traditions. One of these was the tradition of the "plain style," which the Puritans made so much of and which accounts for so much of the strength of the Puritan literature.

The paragraph develops in detail how this Puritan tradition led to advertising that is natural and simple.

### Use Analogy

Analogy develops an idea by comparing it with a similar idea. It is important to choose a comparison object or idea that will be familiar to your reader.

> Being discriminated against when applying for a job because of the colour of one's hair is like being discriminated against for the colour of one's shoes: both are arbitrary and bear no relation to one's ability to do the job.

## Transitions Between and Within Paragraphs

Although your paragraphs will be self-contained, they must interlock to produce a strong argument. Transitions both between and within paragraphs are essential to the flow of your ideas.

### Transitions Between Paragraphs

The most important transitions come between paragraphs. Try to establish a connection between the first sentence of a new paragraph and the last sentence of the preceding one. A linking word may be the easiest way:

> *Thus,* the pattern established by Dickens in the first chapter is consistent throughout the rest of the first volume.
>
> *However*, volume 2 offers a new approach to the narrative . . .

The echo of a key phrase or word can also be effective.

> **End of paragraph:** Whatever Lear's faults, one cannot deny that he *loves* his daughters.
>
> **Beginning of next paragraph:** However, *love* counts for little in the realm of Regan and Goneril.

Be aware that echoing the preceding sentence too closely will result in repetition rather than transition. Here is an unsuccessful attempt to link the introduction to the body of the essay:

> **End of paragraph:** The other important function Bottom has is his major contribution to the humorous aspect of the play.
>
> **Beginning of next paragraph:** For example, one of the major functions of Bottom is his contribution to the play's humour.

### Transitional Sentences

A transition may require a complete sentence.

> **End of paragraph:** The evidence suggests that there is no other option.
>
> **Beginning of next paragraph:** *And yet there may be a solution.* If you disregard the obvious difficulties, you can see that the crow could theoretically open the box if it were to insert its beak at an angle and twist its head to the right.

A transitional sentence does not indicate what will come next in the paragraph; instead, it establishes how the coming paragraph is related to the last. Note that a transitional sentence displaces the topic sentence from its position at the beginning of a paragraph; the topic sentence should directly follow the transitional sentence in this case.

### Transitional Paragraphs

Generally speaking, a transitional paragraph is used in a longer essay, where the essay has been broken into two or more sections. In such essays, each section would be composed of multiple paragraphs. (Imagine each of your paragraphs as an essay within an essay.)

There are two forms of transitional paragraphs. One is shorter; it indicates both visually and in words that you are transitioning between ideas. The other is a regular-length body paragraph, expressly describing how you will shift between sections. These paragraphs often take the opportunity to conclude your point and reorient your reader toward the coming section.

> So far, I have pointed to two areas which I see as characteristic, or at least instructive, of the nature of Canadian poetry. The third and final area I would like to look at is the Canadian preference for the long poem. Here I would argue that the "double voicing" takes the form ...

## Paragraph Length

The question of how long a paragraph should be is hard to answer. The best way of determining paragraph length is to ask, "Does this paragraph say what it should?" rather than "Is this paragraph long enough?" As your writing improves, you will discover that length is determined by your topic and purpose rather than by rules.

There are two considerations when determining an appropriate length for an essay paragraph: the first is content; each paragraph should contain a full thought. The second is visual; a paragraph should not cover an entire page. Often, a paragraph that looks too long is too long. As a general rule, essays allow for detailed paragraphs of roughly 150 to 250 words. If your paragraph becomes too long, try to break it into two smaller paragraphs, narrowing your topic sentences to match the specifics of each paragraph.

Paragraphs throughout your paper should be relatively similar in length. This gives each paragraph equal weight in the eyes of the reader, and it helps you to produce a fully developed argument for each point.

# WRITING STRONG SENTENCES

Strong sentences focus your reader on the points you want to make and reduce the chances that your reader will become confused or lose track of what you are saying. The following suggestions will help you develop your skill in crafting concise, clear, and readable sentences that communicate your ideas effectively.

## Use Strong, Clear Subjects and Verbs

The subject of the sentence is the person or thing that is being described or is doing the action in the sentence. In the sentence "The statistics are persuasive," *the statistics* is the subject. Verbs are words that describe an action or a state. So, in the example sentence, *are* is the verb.

When your sentences use weak subjects and verbs, they miss the chance to focus the reader's attention on the real topic of the sentences. For example, in the following sentences, the focus is on the unimportant phrases (called *empty subjects*) *there are* and *it is*.

> There are three factors that contributed to the final results.

> It is crucial for Mary to consider the consequences of her actions.

Ask yourself, What is the real topic of each sentence? Where do I want my reader to focus? *Three factors* and *Mary* are much stronger subjects.

> Three factors contributed to the final results.

> Mary must consider the consequences of her actions.

Go through your draft to identify places where you have used weak subjects and verbs. Empty subjects are not grammatically incorrect, and there are times when they are the best choice (as in this clause), but they should not be a dominant feature of your writing.

## Choose the Right Voice

English has two voices: **active** and **passive**. Both are grammatical, but they produce very different effects in your writing, depending on how you use them. Consider the following two sentences.

> The student wrote the report yesterday.

> The report was written yesterday.

These two sentences are both about a student, a report, and when the report was written. The first sentence is written in the active voice. The subject of the sentence (*the student*) is the actor, so we assume that the information about who wrote the report is most important. The second sentence is written in the passive voice. The subject of the sentence is the report, so we assume that the report is more important than who wrote it or when.

Some academic writing favours the passive voice because it appears more objective. However, the passive voice can make a sentence confusing. In addition, the passive voice can send the message that you are not confident in your writing. Do not use passive voice to avoid taking responsibility for or ownership of your ideas. Tell the reader who did what. (Notice also that passive sentences are wordier.) Consider these passive-voice sentences.

> The trees were cut down.

> It is argued that cats make better pets than dogs.

With these types of sentences, the reader is left wondering who cut down the trees and who is doing the arguing. In the revised sentences below, the reader knows exactly who the important actors were and what they did.

> Municipal workers cut down the trees.

> I argue (*or* This paper argues) that cats make better pets than dogs.

## Construct Parallel Sentences and Paragraphs

Parallel sentences contribute to the flow of a paper, while non-parallel sentences make a paper awkward and difficult to read. Parallel structure demonstrates that concepts and ideas have the same level of importance; it results when all the grammatical elements (nouns, verbs, adjectives, adverbs, clauses, and so on) in a sentence match. These elements are usually joined by *and, or,* or *but.*

| | |
|---|---|
| Not parallel | The meal was cold, dry, and had no flavour. |
| Parallel | The meal was cold, dry, and flavourless. |
| Not parallel | The doctor told Frank to stop smoking, to eat better, and that he had to lose twenty pounds. |
| Parallel | The doctor told Frank to stop smoking, to eat better, and to lose twenty pounds. |

Parallelism also applies to comparison and contrast. When you are comparing or contrasting two items (for example, people, things, statements, actions), make sure they are in the same category and on the same level.

| | |
|---|---|
| Not Parallel: | Sound travels faster in water than air. |
| Parallel | Sound travels faster in water than in air. |
| | or |
| | Sound travels faster in water than it does in air. |

## Vary Your Sentence Structures

Pay attention to your sentence structures when you are writing and when you revise. Are all the sentences structured the same way? Have you used sentence patterns that include transitions like *however, therefore, moreover,* and *in addition* repeatedly throughout your paragraph? This pattern, when repeated, gives your writing a jerky flow. Take this passage as an example:

> People commonly believe that they should learn another language when they are young. However, that is not always the case. Therefore, anyone can start learning a new language any time. Moreover, the method one uses to learn a new language is important. Therefore, finding a method that works just right for you is essential to the success of your language learning.

The above sentences use the same sentence structure repeatedly. The result is not only difficult to read but also unclear. Try this instead:

> People commonly believe that they should learn another language when they are young, but that is not always the case. Anyone can start learning a new language any time. However, the method one uses to learn a new language is important, so learners must find a method that works just right for them to ensure the success of language learning.

Use a combination of short, medium, and long sentences. When used sparingly, short sentences can have a strong impact on the reader. Likewise, the occasional long sentence can be impressive. When sentences are similar in pattern or are of similar length, your writing will lack interest and strength.

## Keep Subject and Verb Together

Take a look at your sentences. Underline the subject of the sentence and put a box around the verb. They should be right next to each other.

| | |
|---|---|
| Apart | The participant, in addition to completing the survey, agreed to a follow-up interview. |
| Together | The participant agreed to complete the survey and a follow-up interview. |

## Put the Verb Near the Beginning of the Sentence

Readers usually look for the subject and the verb of a sentence, so it is helpful to put them closer to the beginning of the sentence.

**Verb at the end of the sentence:** Unfortunately, because few people responded to the survey, the results were invalid.

**Verb nearer the beginning of the sentence:** Unfortunately, the results were invalid because few people responded to the survey.

## Write Concise Sentences

Writing concisely means using as few words as necessary to convey your meaning. Unnecessary words distract readers and detract from the strength of your argument. Concise wording focuses readers on what is important.

Academic writing often uses long sentences, but longer is not necessarily better. Compare the following sentences. Notice all the unnecessary words in the first.

| | |
|---|---|
| Wordy | The purpose of this research is to evaluate the degree of effectiveness of the current system. |
| Concise | This research evaluates the current system's effectiveness. |

Here are some ways to avoid wordiness.

### Eliminate Unnecessary Determiners and Modifiers

When used appropriately, modifiers and determiners add strength and clarity to your writing. However, they are often unnecessary and can be eliminated. Those that should be removed where possible include the following:

| | |
|---|---|
| *actually* | *basically* |
| *generally* | *definitely* |
| *kind of* | *sort of* |

As you edit your writing, decide whether the determiners and modifiers you have used are necessary. If not, omit them.

Try not to use words like *obviously*, *apparently*, or *absolutely*. Something may be obvious or apparent to you, but it may not be to your reader.

### Avoid Repetitive Wording

Pay attention to your sentences and paragraphs. If there is a word of phrase you use over and over, remove or modify it. Compare the following:

| Original | Three methods have been introduced to deal with the rabbit overpopulation problem on UVic's campus. The first method is to trap, to capture, and to euthanize the rabbits. The second method is to develop a rabbit-free zone and a rabbit zone throughout campus. The third method is to create a rabbit adoption program to adopt out the rabbits to local families and individuals in the community. |
| --- | --- |
| Revised | Three methods have been introduced to deal with rabbit overpopulation at UVic: first, to trap, capture, and euthanize the rabbits; second, to develop rabbit and rabbit-free zones on campus; and third, to find new homes for the rabbits in the community. |

### Omit Redundant Pairs or Categories

Modifiers are redundant when they are used with nouns that do not need modification. Check your writing for redundant modifiers like the following:

* *period in time* (a period and a time are the same thing)
* *past history* (history is always in the past)
* *return back* (when you return, you go back; you needn't say both)
* *red in colour* (red is a colour and can only be a colour)
* *future plans* (plans are always for the future)
* *share in common* (anything shared is in common; you needn't say both)
* *square in shape* (square is a shape)

### Don't Overuse Adjectives

Don't use two descriptive words when one will do. If you want to make a distinction between the two words, make sure it is clear by adding more information to the sentence or changing one of the words.

| Confusing | The study proved that people who are active and exercise are healthier than those who do not. |
| --- | --- |
| Less confusing | The study proved that people who are physically active are healthier than those who are not.<br>*or*<br>The study proved that people who are socially and physically active are healthier than those who are not. |

### Replace Unnecessary Phrases

Replace phrases with single adjectives where possible.

| Original | Students <u>with qualifications</u> were selected. |
| --- | --- |
| Revised | <u>Qualified</u> students were selected. |

## Construct Your Sentences Correctly

Your sentences will be easier to read, and therefore more effective, if they are correctly constructed. The most common problems with sentence construction are incomplete sentences (called **sentence fragments**) and incorrectly joined sentences (**comma splices** and **run-on sentences**). To learn how to avoid or correct these problems, see "Common Errors in Grammar" on page 134.

# USING WORDS EFFECTIVELY

The actual words you choose to express your ideas—your **diction**—make a great difference in how your ideas are received. In academic writing, your words should reflect the right level of formality, make your writing concise and clear, and be objective and unbiased. Many of the ways you use language in everyday life are not found in academic English. These include slang (words like *dude* and *awesome*), non-standard forms (words like *gonna* or *ain't*), and other forms of casual, informal language.

As a university student, you will be expected to use standard Canadian English. While different people may interpret *standard* in different ways, you can think of it as the type of English you read in most published works, including newspapers, magazines, and non-fiction books. You can get an idea of the academic language you should use by examining the language used in textbooks, journals, and other types of academic writing.

Here are some suggestions for how to use words more effectively in your academic writing.

## Use the Appropriate Level of Formality

Writing can be divided into two major styles: **formal** and **informal**. Formal language, the style used in most academic writing, is impersonal, precise, and carefully constructed. Informal language, the style you use in conversation and in non-academic writing, such as personal letters or online postings, is less concerned with correctness and may use shorter sentences, simpler punctuation, and slang or colloquial words and expressions.

Most essays, reports, and other longer forms of writing for university will require you to write in formal English. Here are some tips for ensuring that your writing has the right level of formality.

### Avoid Contractions

One of the easiest ways to create a sense of formality in your writing is to avoid contractions, words like *can't, wouldn't, didn't,* and *you've*. Contractions are commonly used in spoken English and in informal writing, including most journalism, but they may not be acceptable in your academic writing. To be on the safe side, avoid contractions or ask your instructor whether they will be accepted in your written assignments.

### Use Formal Diction

Academic writing uses precise, often specialized, words. The language you will be expected to use in your formal academic writing demands more care and attention than the language you use when talking or writing informally.

Formal academic writing has the following characteristics:

- It uses specialized terminology (words like *phoneme, geomagnetism, spectroscopy,* or *multicollinearity*). When you write within your discipline, you will be expected to use the specialized terms of the discipline in your writing.

- It avoids informal, colloquial, or slang words and expressions.
- It uses single words rather than phrases (for example, *require* instead of *have to get*).
- It uses an educated general vocabulary (for example, words like *criteria, context, variable, proportionate, continuum, hypothesize,* or *preclude*). Many are abstract words that you will need both to comprehend and use in your formal writing.

Mastering formal diction is part of general vocabulary building. Your vocabulary will increase as you read and study. For help with expanding your vocabulary, see "Building Your Academic Vocabulary" on page 26.

## Use the Correct Person

**Person** is the term used in grammar to distinguish between the writer or speaker (first person), the listener or reader (second person), and the person or thing being talked or written about (third person). In English, personal pronouns are divided into these three categories:

| | |
|---|---|
| first person | *I, we, me, us, my, our, mine, ours* |
| second person | *you, your, yours* |
| third person | *he, him, his, she, her, hers, it, its, they, them, their, theirs* |

Most academic writing uses **third person**, which reflects the impersonal, objective style of formal English. Some assigned work may require you to use first person (for example, personal reflections, first-person narratives, or personal essays). If you are in doubt, check with your instructor.

Here are some special considerations in the use of person in your writing:

**we:** Some people treat *we* as an acceptable alternative to using third person. For example, "In Canada, *we* have an abundance of freshwater." However, unless *we* refers to an identified group that the reader is aware of, use third person instead: "*Canada* has an abundance of freshwater."

**you:** In spoken English, *you* is often used as a generic pronoun meaning *one*. For example, "If climate change continues, *you* will see a rise in sea levels." Unless *you* refers to your reader, avoid it in academic writing. You may have to rewrite the sentence: "If climate change continues, *sea levels* will rise."

**he:** In spoken English, *they* or *their* is often used to refer to a third-person singular subject. For example, "If a *participant* in the study did not complete the questionnaire, *they* were sent a reminder." But *participant* is singular, and *they* is a plural pronoun. While the use of *they* and *their* as first-person pronouns is common in spoken English, it is still frowned upon in formal writing. Here are three ways to fix the problem:

- **Use he or she (or other combination, as appropriate):**
  If a *participant* in the study did not complete the questionnaire, *he or she* was sent a reminder.

- **Make the subject plural:**
  If *participants* in the study did not complete the questionnaire, *they* were sent a reminder.

- **Reword the sentence:**
  *Participants* in the study who did not complete the questionnaire were sent a reminder.

## Use Exact Words

The more exact your wording, the clearer your meaning will be. Choose words that capture your ideas precisely.

### Denotation and Connotation

Sometimes, you use a word that is technically correct, but your meaning is skewed by the *connotations* the word has. You should be aware of both a word's **denotation** and **connotation** before you use it.

- **Denotation** refers to a word's literal meaning.
- **Connotation** refers to the associations, or "shades of meaning," that a word has.

For example, the words *thrifty* and *penny-pinching* share much of the same meaning, or denotation, but they have very different connotations. *Thrifty* suggests spending money wisely rather than wasting it, whereas *penny-pinching* suggests miserliness or excessive concern about money.

As a critical reader and writer, you should always be considering how connotation influences meaning. Consider, for example, how your response to a newspaper story changes depending on whether a person is referred to as a *terrorist* or as a *freedom fighter*, as a *soldier* or as a *peacekeeper*.

Be careful when you choose words. Be aware of their connotations. A dictionary definition will include both a word's denotation and its connotations, so be sure to read the whole entry. You can use a thesaurus to find a synonym that better captures your meaning, if needed.

### General Words and Specific Words

**General words** are used to indicate broad categories of things. **Specific words** name specific members of broad categories.

| General | dog | hat | worker | vegetable |
|---|---|---|---|---|
| Specific | English spaniel | beret | legal secretary | eggplant |

General words are useful for stating general truths or for making broad statements, but you need specific words to express specific ideas. You should choose specific words over general words. Much of the vocabulary you learn at university is highly specific. Your ability to use the precise word called for in a given context represents your mastery of the discipline.

### Concrete Words and Abstract Words

**Concrete words** name things that can be experienced by your five senses; you can see, hear, smell, touch, or taste them: *fox, thunder, ammonia, silky,* and *peppery* are concrete words.

**Abstract words** name concepts, ideas, theories, and other things that have no con-crete representation: *beautiful, initiative, society, evolving,* and *contempt* are abstract words.

Abstract words are common in academic writing, which is mainly concerned with concepts, ideas, and theories. But too much abstraction makes your writing hard to understand, especially for readers who are not familiar with the abstractions you are discussing.

If your writing contains mostly general and abstract words, your meaning may not be clear to your reader. Be careful to balance these words with concrete and specific words that clarify your meaning, or define your use of an abstract term so that readers understand how you are using it.

## Avoid Common Word-Choice Problems

Just as good word choice strengthens your writing, poor word choice weakens your writing. Here are some common problems:

### Weak Verbs

Choose clear, strong verbs that express an action. Verbs like *examine, combine, allow, emphasize,* or *divide* tell the reader in a single word what action is being described. Avoid weak uses of *to be* (*is, are, was, were*) by creating active sentences:

| | |
|---|---|
| Weak (passive) | The conclusion of the committee <u>was</u> that the plan should be revised. |
| Strong (active) | The committee <u>concluded</u> that the plan should be revised. |

Other weak verbs (*come, make, take, have*) appear in common phrases that can be replaced by a single verb, like the following:

| | |
|---|---|
| *take into consideration* | *consider* |
| *make a decision* | *decide* |
| *come to an agreement* | *agree* |
| *take a vote* | *vote* |

### Noun Forms of Verbs

In English, it is easy to turn a verb into a noun. The resulting noun is abstract and often makes the sentence longer or harder to read. These words often end in *–tion* or *–ment,* among others. You can often make your sentence clearer and simpler by turning nomi-nalizations back into the verbs they came from. For example:

| | |
|---|---|
| Original | The purpose of this project is the <u>exploration</u> of how <u>improvements</u> to the current patient data system could save lives. |
| Revised | This project <u>explores</u> how <u>improving</u> the current patient data system could save lives. |

### Clichés

Clichés are sayings or phrases that are too commonly used and have lost some of their impact because of their familiarity. Clichés to avoid in academic writing include:

| | |
|---|---|
| *easier said than done* | *slowly but surely* |
| *few and far between* | *in this day and age* |

| | |
|---|---|
| *last but not least* | *for all intents and purposes* |
| *beyond the shadow of a doubt* | *hit the nail on the head* |
| *tried and true* | *better late than never* |

## Use Inclusive Language

Language can exclude or offend particular groups. Learning to avoid biased language requires attention to how your words might be objectionable or hurtful to readers.

### General Guidelines

■ Don't refer to a person's sex, skin colour, culture, religion, sexual orientation, age, level of income, or physical or mental disability unless it is directly relevant to the discussion.

■ Watch for stereotypes in your writing, such as assuming that particular jobs are done by women (nurse, kindergarten teacher) or by men (engineer, CEO, carpenter), that particular ethnic or religious groups think or act a particular way, or that a person's sexual orientation, physical ability, or other characteristic makes him or her likely to be or act in a particular way.

■ If you aren't sure whether a term is offensive, ask your instructor for guidance or ask someone from the group you think you might offend. To learn more about words that might offend, a quick search for "biased language" will lead you to many web pages on the topic.

### Gendered Language

Sexist language is the most common form of biased language because it is built into English. Until recently, words like *chairman, manpower,* and *forefathers* had no gender-neutral equivalent. Today we use the neutral words *chair* (or *chairperson*), *labour,* and *ancestors* in their place.

Here are some other replacements for common gender-specific terms:

| | |
|---|---|
| *mankind* | *humanity, people* |
| *sportsmanship* | *fair play* |
| *mothering* | *parenting* |
| *man of the house* | *head of the household* |
| *wears the pants* | *holds the power* |
| *businessman* | *businessperson* |
| *policeman* | *police officer* |
| *statesman* | *politician, political leader* |
| *man in the street, average Joe* | *average person* |

In academic writing, titles such as *Mr., Mrs., Miss,* and *Ms.* are rarely used. However, if you use *Mr.* to refer to a man, use *Ms.* to refer to a woman. *Mr.* and *Ms.* are parallel because neither reveals the person's marital status.

Do not use *he* as the generic third-person pronoun. (For example, "The average Canadian is worried about his future.") Either use *he and she* (or *she and he*) or revise the sentence, as suggested earlier in this section.

# Part II: Common Academic Writing Assignments

# UNDERSTANDING YOUR ASSIGNMENT

Each academic assignment you are given will ask you to demonstrate your learning in specific ways—ways that you might feel aren't very clear. By spending time carefully reading and analyzing the assignment instructions themselves, you will have a clearer idea of what your instructor expects—and a better chance of doing well.

## Consider the Purpose of the Assignment

The first thing to identify in your assignment is what you are being asked to *do*. If you focus on what you have to produce (for example, an essay, a paper, or a report), you risk overlooking what your essay, paper, or report actually has to demonstrate.

### Pay Attention to Verbs

Here are some of the common verbs you will encounter in your academic assignments along with explanations of what they are directing you to do.

#### Argue

You are being asked to take a position, often on a controversial subject, and to persuade your reader of that position by presenting your reasons for your position, supported by evidence. The keys to a successful argument are a strong thesis and strong supporting evidence. (Assignments that tell you to defend an idea or support your opinion usually expect you to argue.)

#### Analyze

You are being asked to take something apart (usually a written work, theory, event, or similar object of academic study) and to examine its parts. Regardless of how simple or complex the subject of your analysis is, the process is the same: divide it into its parts, examine each part in turn, and consider how the parts relate to one another. Often, you will be asked to analyze in order to discuss or argue the merits and faults of whatever it is you are analyzing. (Assignments that ask you to interpret a literary text usually expect you to analyze and then discuss or argue.)

#### Compare

You are being asked to analyze two or more things (e.g., processes, texts, approaches) and to describe how they are the same and how they are different. The implication in being asked to compare two (or more) things is that you should determine their relative merits. You will need to argue to show which of the things you are analyzing is the best and why it is the best.

#### Describe

You are being asked to identify the most important features or characteristics of something. The secret to a successful description is to pay attention to even the smallest of details. Then, think about which are most relevant to the writing situation and audience and select those you will feature in your description. (Assignments that tell you to report on or show something usually want you to describe.)

#### Explain

You are being asked to describe something and then offer reasons for why it is the way it is. It is not uncommon to be asked to explain a historical or mechanical process or an operation; try to break such actions, whether they are mental or physical, into steps, and describe them one at a time. (An assignment that asks you to provide reasons usually requires that you explain.)

*Discuss*

You are being asked to carefully and thoughtfully consider a topic in order to show your understanding of it. A discussion usually includes a detailed presentation of the main points and details of the subject matter. If you are asked to discuss a controversy, question, or argument, you will want to offer some consideration of the pros and cons, supported by examples and other evidence. (Assignments that ask you to report on or review or demonstrate knowledge of a topic are often directing you to discuss.)

*Recommend*

You are being asked to put forward a solution or a course of action in response to a problem. Usually, a situation that requires a recommendation suggests that more than one answer is possible. You should therefore not only give a detailed analysis of your own idea but also explain why it is the best among those that are possible. Is it the most efficient? Is it the fastest? Is it the cheapest? Is it the most beneficial? Why should your idea be the one used? (Note that assignments that ask you to suggest or propose usually expect you to recommend.)

## Other Questions to Ask

After you have determined what you are being asked to do, it is important to identify the rest of the details.

- ✓ Is the topic or scope limited in some way?
- ✓ What kinds of sources am I being asked to refer to? Am I limited to academic, print sources only, or can I use online materials, popular media, or my own experiences as evidence?
- ✓ How many sources do I have to use?
- ✓ Is there a page or word limit?
- ✓ Is a particular format required?
- ✓ Is a particular citation style required?
- ✓ When is it due?

Sometimes, even after you have carefully deconstructed the components of your assignment, you still have questions. In this case, don't be afraid to contact your instructor for clarification.

The following example shows how the above questions would be applied to an assignment.

### The Assignment

The incidence of bedbug infestations on the south coast of BC has increased markedly in the last few years. Citing evidence from at least four course readings and at least two additional sources, provide reasons for this increase and suggest some strategies for controlling these infestations. Your essay should not exceed 1,500 words and should be presented on 8.5 x 11-inch paper, using one-inch margins and 12-point Times New Roman font. It is due at midnight on March 15.

### What is this purpose of the assignment?

To _explain_ why bedbug infestations have increased recently in BC in southern coastal areas; to _recommend_ strategies for controlling these infestations; to _discuss_ the topic in a way that demonstrates knowledge and understanding of my course readings and outside sources.

### Is the topic or scope limited in some way?

I am only asked to write about recent bedbug infestations in south coastal BC.

### What kinds of texts am I being asked to refer to? Do I need to only refer to academic sources?

Both class reading and outside readings. I can refer to sources that are not academic, but it seems like it would be best to stick to academic sources that are like our class readings.

### How many texts do I have to use?

Minimum: 4 class readings and 2 outside sources. No maximum

### Is there a page or word limit?

1,500 words (so write 1,400 to 1,600 words)

### Is a particular format required?

8.5 x 11-inch paper
one-inch margins
12-point Times New Roman font

### Is a particular citation style required?

None is given. I need to check the syllabus or ask my instructor.

### What is the deadline?

Midnight, March 15; I think that means I need to submit the essay through the class Moodle site, but I'll check with the instructor to make sure.

## Revising and Checking

After you have finished writing a complete draft of your essay, go back through the assignment and check that your work fulfills all the assignment requirements. Have you done what you were asked to _do_, not just created what you were asked to produce? Have you addressed the question asked? Does your essay cover all of the components mentioned in the assignment? (For instance, the assignment example above should lead you to double-check that you have explained _why_ the above-mentioned bedbug infestations have been occurring and _how_ their frequency might be reduced.)

Sometimes, students address too much. Have you limited your discussion to what has been asked, or have you strayed from the topic? (For the example assignment, you should limit your analysis to bedbug infestations that have _happened recently on the southern BC coast_. If you write a history of bedbug infestation around the world or a long description of the signs of bedbug infestation, you have strayed from the topic.)

Make sure that you have used at least the minimum number of sources and no more than the maximum. Also ensure that you have complied with the page or word limit. (For the example assignment, you should make certain that the text of the essay refers to at least four course readings and two outside readings. You would also want to check that your essay isn't much more than 1,500 words and that it is in 12-point, Times New Roman font.)

## Other Considerations

### Who is the Audience?

Related to the purpose of the assignment is its audience. For whom are you asked to write? The assignment may be a proposal you present to a potential business partner, or it may be a lab report that provides details of a scientific experiment for a teaching assistant (TA). Usually when an assignment doesn't specify target readers, you should imagine an educated, academic audience; your instructor represents that audience. Keeping your audience in mind helps you to decide how formal the tone or language of your essay should be. It also suggests whether technical terms need to be explained and basic background information needs to be offered.

### What Format or Structure Are You Required to Use?

✔ How many paragraphs or sections are required, if specified?

✔ Are you allowed to use point form?

✔ Are you expected to use headings and subheadings?

✔ Does your assignment have to follow a specific structure?

### What Sources Are You Required to Use?

✔ From where have you been asked to draw your sources?

✔ Are you required to use primary and secondary sources?

✔ Do sources have to be peer-reviewed?

✔ Are you supposed to use specific articles from course texts, reserve readings, or a course website?

✔ Do you need to find your own sources?

✔ Do you need to use some print sources as well as some electronic sources?

✔ Can you use sources other than online library databases to diversify your evidence?

### How Will You Be Graded?

Most instructors include a grading scheme either with the written assignment instructions or as part of the course syllabus. Review grading criteria carefully to determine the most important aspects of your assignment. The elements of the assignment that will count most heavily towards the overall grade are the ones you should spend the most time researching, drafting, and editing.

## DEVELOPING A THESIS

All academic papers need a **thesis**: the main idea, or point, that the rest of the paper explores and supports. A strong thesis gives your paper a focus, which will help direct your ideas and reinforce your purposes as you write.

If you are writing a research paper, your thesis should state your approach to a research question. If you are writing without research, your thesis should be the result of your reflection upon either the work you are writing about or a question that has been posed. In either case, your essay develops evidence to support your thesis.

### Formulating Your Thesis

A good way to begin developing your thesis is by thinking closely about a topic until you find a question you want to address or a puzzle you want to explore. Think of your thesis as your answer to that question or your solution to the puzzle. Sometimes, you will need to do more research in order to formulate your question; again, you want to pay attention to puzzles, contradictions, and problems that seem not to be adequately explained, or topics you want to know more about.

Consider the following examples:

> You have been asked to write about the use of propaganda in Nazi Germany. You observe that the Germans in posters from the time are often depicted as tall, muscular, and blonde, but you know that Hitler was short, plump, and dark-haired. You decide to write on the discrepancy between the ideal German as shown in Nazi propaganda and Hitler, the leader of the party. This discrepancy leads to the question "Why was the ideal German of the propaganda so different from the physical appearance of the Nazi leader?" All your further research would be guided by this question. In the process of your research, you discover that Hitler disliked his own appearance.
>
> **Your thesis:** *The propaganda of the Nazi party reflected the physical insecurities of its leader, Adolph Hitler.*
>
> Your professor asks you to discuss the one recent or pending change to economic policy that will most affect Canada's competitive advantage. As part of your exploratory research, you come across a website that lists the free trade agreement between the US and Canada (NAFTA) as a source of competitive advantages for Canadian companies. You research pending free trade agreements and discover that negotiations on free trade between Canada and the European Union are scheduled for early 2011. Your research question might be "How would a free trade agreement between Canada and the EU affect Canada's competitive advantage?" In the process of researching the answer to this question, you discover research that suggest that freer trade is economically beneficial.
>
> **Your thesis:** *If Canada successfully negotiates free trade with the EU, the treaty will offer new business opportunities to all provinces and further diversify an economy that still depends heavily on the United States as a main trading partner, greatly increasing the competitive advantage of companies in Canada.*

## Writing Your Thesis Statement

Once you have developed a thesis, sharpen it into a concise statement. The **thesis statement** usually appears in the introductory paragraph of your essay, often (but not necessarily) as the paragraph's final sentence. This definition of your position or declaration of the point you intend to prove is often best expressed in one sentence.

## Refining Your Thesis Statement

A good thesis statement takes work. You might begin your research with a tentative answer to your research question. As you research, you will likely revise your answer. Even as you are writing your essay, you might still be refining your interpretation of your research. Keep checking that your thesis captures the main point of your essay.

As you work on refining your thesis, check that your thesis does not suffer from one of the following common problems:

- a thesis that is too obvious to be worth arguing (called a *truism*)
- a thesis that is too broad to be proven
- a thesis that is too narrow for the scope of your assignment
- a thesis that is vague or off topic

Here are examples of thesis statements, good and bad, written for two essay topics:

### Topic: *The decline in reading among young Canadians*

**Too obvious:** *Young Canadians don't read much.*

**Too broad:** *The decline in literacy parallels a decline in civilization.*

**Vague:** *Reading is important for the development of social values.*

**A good thesis:** *As young Canadians spend more time playing computer games they have less time available for reading.*

**A better thesis:** *To get an accurate picture of the reading habits of young Canadians, researchers need to include the reading done online by young people, not just their reading of print books and newspapers.*

### Topic: *The purpose of Bottom's character in A Midsummer Night's Dream*

**Too obvious:** *The purpose of Bottom is to be humorous.*

**Too narrow:** *Bottom's name is a pun that refers to his head.*

**Vague:** *Shakespeare often uses humorous characters like Bottom in comedies.*

**Off-topic:** *Bottom is a funny name for a character in Shakespeare.*

**A good thesis:** *Bottom links the mortal and immortal realms.*

**A better thesis:** *Bottom, the only mortal character to cross into the immortal realm, personifies humour's immortality, suggesting that Shakespearean comedy can be even more substantial than tragedy.*

# WRITING AN ESSAY

**Essays** come in many different forms and lengths, and are called by many different names, including the research paper, critical analysis, close reading, rhetorical analysis, review, and report. Underlying all these genres of academic writing are the same basic purpose, structure, and process.

## Why Essay Writing Matters

A well-written essay shows your engagement with your learning and contributes to the development of knowledge—the purpose of all academic writing. It will show your instructor that you are able to

- read and understand assigned material and the works referred to in your paper
- conduct research (if required)
- critique material and offer fresh insights into a topic
- generate an original argument and prove your points through reasoning and evidence (such as quotes and data)
- organize your argument logically and persuasively
- cite sources appropriately and correctly
- write clearly and correctly

When you are assigned an essay, your task is not simply to review information on a topic and make observations. Neither is it to summarize the arguments of others. To write a good essay, you must generate ideas and arguments of your own.

## The Essay-Writing Process

Before you begin writing an essay, you should understand your purpose and consider your audience. These are the first steps in any writing project and are described in detail in ""Understanding Your Assignment" on page 78.

In order to write a well-organized essay, you will need to

- choose and narrow your topic
- determine your stance
- write an effective thesis statement
- develop your evidence
- create an outline
- draft your essay
- revise

### Choosing and Narrowing Your Topic

Your **topic** is the subject of your essay, the theme you will discuss, or the problem you will solve. A topic can be broad or narrow.

| Broad Topic | Narrow Topic |
| --- | --- |
| Global warming | the effect of global warming on the ice sheet in Greenland |
| Social welfare | the development of child welfare laws in post-WWII Canada |
| Film history | the representation of nature in the early films of Akira Kurosawa |

Often, your instructor will assign a topic or will offer a range of topics to choose from. In the latter case, pick the topic that interests you most. In either case, narrow the topic so that it is specific.

Read about your topic (including all readings on the topic assigned in class). Search for information about your topic in the library and online.

As you read, ask yourself

✓ What do others think about this topic?

✓ How has thinking on this subject changed over time?

✓ What do I think about what others have said?

✓ Are there flaws or gaps in the reasoning of the writers I am reading?

✓ Are there points they may have missed or points of view they have ignored?

Write down your thoughts as you read. Through this process, you will discover your ideas on your topic, which will lead you to your thesis. Summarizing what you read can also help you develop your supporting points.

Try some of these other activities to generate ideas for writing:

- Discuss and brainstorm ideas with others.
- Draw a diagram to represent your ideas.
- Write down all the ideas that come to mind about your topic.

For more suggestions on developing a topic and other research activities, see "Defining a Good Research Topic" on page 29.

## Determining Your Stance

Decide on the stance you will take. Some topics, especially controversial topics (abortion, capital punishment, euthanasia), will make you think of obvious stances, for and against. With other topics, it may be less obvious that there is a position to be taken.

Look at the sample essay questions below and try asking yourself the following questions: Do I agree with one perspective more than with another? Which point of view could I support most convincingly?

Describe the development of astronomy during the European Renaissance. Which astronomer—Kepler, Galileo, or Brahe—made the most important contribution to modern astronomy?

"Students in the arts often have difficulty with mathematics, while science students tend to write poorly." Is this a stereotype? Why or why not?

For the first example, you will have to decide what is meant by "important"; otherwise, you will not know what position you should take. For the second, you will have to decide whether you think the idea is a stereotype or not and why. Do you think that all students write poorly, whether or not they are in the sciences, or do you believe that most science students do a degree in the sciences because they have trouble with writing?

## Writing an Effective Thesis Statement

The essence of every essay is its thesis. The thesis is the point your essay is making, the central idea or argument that the rest of the essay develops and supports.

A **thesis statement** is a concise statement of your argument. Usually, your thesis statement appears in your introductory paragraph and is only one sentence long. In longer papers, the thesis may be stated over a few sentences.

A good thesis statement should be specific and should assert a position; it should not just present a fact. For more information on writing an effective thesis, see "Developing a Thesis" on page 82.

## Developing Your Evidence

Your evidence is what supports your thesis. Common types of evidence include

- the ideas of other writers and researchers
- facts
- definitions
- survey results
- models
- experimental data
- statistical data
- interviews
- observations
- theorems and equations
- archival material

If you are researching to find evidence, refer to "Finding Sources" on page 32 for more suggestions about where and how to look.

When you use quotations and data from sources, do not simply place them in your essay; link them to your argument and make the connections between them and your thesis clear.

When you use evidence from any sources, you must cite them. This is true even if you do not quote directly. Citation distinguishes between your ideas and the ideas of others. It also acknowledges the contributions of other researchers and writers. See "Using Sources" on page 40 for more information on correct citation and how to avoid plagiarism.

## Creating an Outline

Creating an outline is an effective way to plan an essay. It will help you identify what you are going to say and in what order. An outline ensures that your organization is clear and makes sense to a reader.

If you use an outline, do not feel that once you have created it, you have to stick with it. As you write, you may think of a better way to structure your essay. Feel free to revise or ignore your outline if it no longer works.

See "Outlining" on page 16 for guidelines on creating an outline.

## Writing Your Essay

Once you have decided on your thesis, evidence, and organization, you have completed the most difficult part of your essay. You are now ready to start writing.

Try not to worry too much about how well you are writing when you first start drafting your essay. You can correct your grammar, mechanics, and punctuation when you are revising your work.

See "Writing Your First Draft" on page 18 for more information on writing strategies.

### Writing the introduction

Your introduction should clearly present your argument and capture your reader's attention. It can be one of the most challenging parts of an essay to write. Many writers find it easiest to write the introduction after they have written the body of the essay.

A good introduction should provide your reader with the following information:

■ **Your topic**: Your topic must be clearly stated as soon as possible in your essay. Your introduction should make clear to the reader what you are writing about and why the topic is important.

■ **Any necessary context:** Your introduction should also include any information necessary for your reader to understand your argument. Consider your audience and decide what information would be most helpful to them. This could include a summary of previous theories or assertions about your topic.

■ **Your thesis:** Your thesis is presented within your introduction, usually at the end.

■ **An outline of your argument:** Long essays often include a brief overview of how the argument is organized.

### Writing the body of the essay

In the body, you develop your argument by discussing each point in detail. Your discussion should

■ **Provide evidence.** Strong evidence proves your argument. Your evidence should directly support your thesis.

■ **Explain each point.** Be sure to explain each point you make and give the reasoning behind the evidence you present. Each point should support and refer back to the main argument embodied in your thesis statement.

■ **Be logical.** The success of your argument rests on its logic. Read "Using Logic" on page 90 to learn about common logic problems.

# Basic Essay Structure

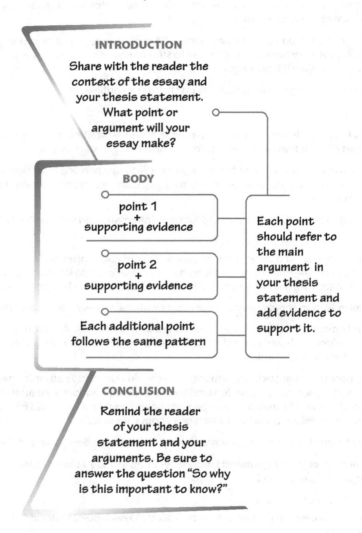

**INTRODUCTION**
Share with the reader the context of the essay and your thesis statement. What point or argument will your essay make?

**BODY**

point 1
+
supporting evidence

point 2
+
supporting evidence

Each additional point follows the same pattern

Each point should refer to the main argument in your thesis statement and add evidence to support it.

**CONCLUSION**
Remind the reader of your thesis statement and your arguments. Be sure to answer the question "So why is this important to know?"

■ **Be coherent.** Clear transitions are essential to the coherence of your argument. Use transitions to connect your ideas so that readers understand how you got from one point to the next.

■ **Be clear.** A clear argument is built of clear sentences and paragraphs. Double-check to make sure your statements follow one another logically and are both connected and easy to follow. You can achieve this by carefully organizing your points. If you aren't sure about your structure, have someone read your essay and point out any places that seem confusing.

Writing the conclusion

A strong conclusion recaps your thesis, connects and summarizes the steps or key points of your argument, ties up any loose ends, and emphasizes your essay's significance. Conclusions work with introductions to frame your paper, and like introductions they can be challenging to write.

If you get stuck, ask yourself, "So what?" You've said all sorts of interesting things. Why did you bother? What was the point? The conclusion is not the place to introduce new evidence or points; it is the place to explain how and why your essay matters.

Avoid simply restating your introduction. The introduction forecasts, while the conclusion sums up. The introduction tells your reader what you are discussing and why. The conclusion states why what you've said is important.

In short, a good conclusion should summarize

■ **What you've said**: Your conclusion should revisit your thesis and synthesize your argument. Do not cut and paste from your introduction. Sum up your argument and consider all that you have said in your essay.

■ **Why you've said it:** Your conclusion is a good place to show why your argument matters in a broader context. For example, if you are writing a history paper, you can include a brief overview of events that were triggered by the issue you examined, or comment on the legacy of the issue in current times.

Other ideas for your conclusion

Conclusions can also include

- any questions for further research in your area of study
- the implications or importance of your work

Compare the main ideas in your conclusion with the main points in your introduction to ensure that you have stayed on topic throughout your essay.

Revising

While revising, ask yourself the following important questions:

- ✔ Have I fulfilled the requirements of the assignment?
- ✔ Does my thesis state my main point?
- ✔ Do my examples clearly relate to my thesis and supporting arguments?
- ✔ Are my ideas clearly connected to one another and to my thesis?
- ✔ Are there any errors in my logic?
- ✔ Is my conclusion a review rather than a simple restatement of my introduction?
- ✔ Are there any grammatical or mechanical errors?
- ✔ Have I cited my sources correctly, both in text and in my references section?

If you are having trouble with your revision, ask a Writing Centre tutor or your instructor for help. When you have finished editing your essay, be sure to proofread it before you hand it in, checking for typos and other minor errors, which may detract from the fluency of your writing or even impede understanding.

# USING LOGIC

In order for an argument to persuade a reader, it must be based in logic. **Logic** is a way of reasoning that draws conclusions from evidence. There are two forms of reasoning: deductive and inductive.

## Deductive Reasoning

**Deductive reasoning** moves from the general to the specific; that is, it derives specific predictions or conclusions from one or more general principles or premises.

*Every time someone kicks a ball, it comes down to earth* states a general principle or premise. *If I kick the ball, it will come down to earth* is a prediction or conclusion based on the premise.

An argument is strong only if the premises are true and the deductions are valid. However, you can have a logical argument but still fail to persuade the reader. In an essay taking the form of argument, you should consider all the evidence, including opposing viewpoints, and have enough examples or detail to make your argument convincing for your audience.

## Inductive Reasoning

**Inductive reasoning** moves from the specific to the general. Arguments that use inductive reasoning move in the opposite direction from deductive arguments. With induction, you derive a general rule from specific cases or situations. If you observe a pattern across enough representative specific cases, your general statement about them is likely to be, but not necessarily, true.

For example, a researcher might observe that many obese children happen to watch a lot of television and inductively conclude that TV is a contributing factor to child obesity. Another researcher might observe that rates of childhood obesity have rapidly increased while the average number of hours children spend watching television has steadily decreased and inductively conclude that TV not strongly linked to child obesity.

Note that complex arguments can include both deductive and inductive reasoning.

## Logical Fallacies

A **logical fallacy** is a flawed argument.

Logical fallacies can be seen or heard almost everywhere—in advertising, on the news, in political debates, in speeches, and in essays. Because you use logic in an essay whenever you make a point, develop an argument, or draw a conclusion, it is important to make sure your arguments are truly valid. Even one flawed argument in an essay will wreck your thesis.

There are many types of logical fallacies. The most common are listed below.

## Invalid Deduction

Invalid deductive reasoning occurs when a conclusion does not follow from the premises, or when one of the premises presented is false or flawed. What appears below is one example of an invalid deduction:

| | |
|---|---|
| Slugs crawl on the ground; | (premise) |
| I can crawl on the ground; | (premise) |
| I am a slug. | (conclusion) |

Here both of the premises are true, but the conclusion doesn't follow from the premises, so the argument is flawed. If you want to learn more about how deductive logic can go wrong, consult a textbook that deals with logic or do an online search.

## Sweeping or Hasty Generalization

Most logical errors related to inductive reasoning arise from the assumption that *some* equals *all*. The fact that the five butterflies you observed were blue doesn't mean that all butterflies are blue.

A **sweeping generalization** arises when you assume that the world at large shares your opinion on a subject. If you write, "Nobody thinks smoking is acceptable," you assume no other opinion is possible. The very existence of smokers suggests that they, at least, do think it acceptable. Qualify and limit your opinion, and you are more likely to make a defensible statement: "Many people find smoking unacceptable."

A **hasty generalization** is an assumption based on incomplete evidence. For example, you would be making a hasty generalization if you concluded after a visit to Vancouver during which the sun shone every day that it is always sunny in Vancouver. You may make a hasty generalization if you assume that something is true based on your experience only.

## Special Pleading

**Special pleading** is a logical fallacy that ignores opposing evidence and uses only evidence that supports a given position. For example, you read about a survey of twenty-five physics students that shows that ninety percent are familiar with Newton's laws of motion. You find another survey that shows most Canadian science students couldn't correctly answer a basic question about Newton's laws of motion. You then argue in your essay that most university students are likely to be familiar with Newton's laws.

## Either/Or

The **either/or argument** assumes that only two alternatives exist when, in reality, there are many more complexities to consider. However, if there really are only two options, you can use an either/or argument safely. For example, if a book is published in only the United States and Canada, you can conclude that anyone owning the book has either the US edition or the Canadian edition. However, if a house falls down in an earthquake, you cannot assume that it fell either because of its weak foundations or a fault in the ground below it—there may be other possible reasons.

### False Analogy

An **analogy** compares one thing to something else. Use analogy to clarify or enhance an argument, but don't mistake it for proof—what is true of one thing in one set of circumstances is not necessarily true of another thing in another set of circumstances.

A **false analogy** makes a weak or misleading comparison between two things whose similarities are not generally recognized. An example of a false analogy would be the comparison of university administrators to Nazis.

### Circular Argument

A **circular argument** restates the premise of the argument in the conclusion. It sounds convincing until you rephrase it and realize that you haven't actually constructed an argument or proven anything. Consider the following examples:

> In *Alice in Wonderland*, the Cheshire Cat tells Alice she must be mad because everyone in Wonderland is mad and she is in Wonderland—therefore, she is mad.

> A mother tells her child to go to bed. When the child asks why, the mother responds, "Because I said so!"

### Distortion of Argument

Misrepresenting or distorting an opponent's claims or arguments can make the argument easier to defeat. Politicians will often accuse their opponents of doing something or saying something that they are not to make people dislike their opponents. For example, a political leader might state, "The opposition will tax you so much that you won't have a house to live in," when in reality, the opposition is proposing to raise one tax and lower another, making no overall difference in the amount of tax being paid.

### Invalidation

This is an argument that presents one answer to a question as if it invalidates all other possible answers. Don't assume that one explanation renders other explanations incorrect; always back up your evidence with facts. Any one or a combination of the explanations might be valid.

### Drawing Invalid or Irrelevant Conclusions

If you base your conclusions on assumed morals, popular opinion, the desire to incite fear in your reader, or personal attacks on those who hold opposing views, your conclusions are neither valid nor relevant, as they are not based on evaluating the terms of the argument itself.

# WRITING A SUMMARY

A **summary** is a highly condensed version of a text that sums up, or distills, the main points of the text into a new and shorter version of the original. A well-written summary has the following characteristics:

- It accurately represents the author's ideas.
- It is shorter than the original.
- It is written in your own words.

Being able to summarize well is essential to academic writing because so much academic writing requires you to summarize and incorporate the ideas of others into your own writing. For example, when you write a research paper, you may have to summarize studies and their results in order to demonstrate a point based on several studies' findings.

Summaries can be long or short:

- A **condensation** is a one-sentence summary.
- A **paraphrase** is one or more sentences that present another writer's ideas in your own words.
- A **précis** is a more formal summary that retains the author's approach and ordering of ideas.

Two common assignments require you to write a summary. You may be asked to summarize a reading. In this case, the entire assignment is your reduction of the reading into its thesis and main points. Your instructor will probably expect you to turn in a précis. You may also need to include a summary of a reading in an essay. If you are using summary within a longer assignment, it is usually best to condense the original unless you need to explain it in more depth.

## How to Write a Summary

■ Understand what you are reading. Read anything you are going to summarize as many times as it takes for you to be able to put the ideas into your own words.

■ Consider the purpose of the summary. Why are you being asked to do it? What, in the context of the assignment, is your summary meant to do or show?

■ Consider the intended audience. Who will be reading the summary? What do they already know? What do they need to know?

■ Highlight the main points the author is making. Identify key sentences by underlining them as you read. Find the thesis statement. Find the topic sentence in each paragraph, section by section.

■ Write down the main points of the article or create a topic sentence outline.

■ Rewrite the main points in your own words. Try to use fewer words—dedicate no more than a sentence to each main point.

■ Be accurate. Your summary must faithfully reproduce the original author's intended meaning. If you are not accurate, you are not summarizing.

■ Provide a full and accurate citation for any text you summarize, using the appropriate documentation style.

■ Using your topic sentence outline, write the summary in your own words. Try not to use any words other than technical terms from the original. If you must use a word or a phrase from the original (other than technical terms), use quotation marks, though normally quotations are best avoided in summaries.

## Tips for Writing Summaries

Below are some tips for writing good summaries:

- Omit or drastically condense lengthy details, examples, and statistics—but do not omit information or examples that are necessary to a clear understanding of the summarized work.

- Be concise: use as few words as possible.

- Preserve the relative emphases of the original, giving more prominence to a point treated at length than to one mentioned in passing.

- Avoid rehashing the author's words. Instead, read, pause, and ask yourself, What did I read? What is the author saying? This approach will help you to summarize in your own words and avoid producing a series of disconnected sentences.

## Sample Summary

Original Passage   The invention of the process of printing from movable type, which occurred in Germany about the middle of the fifteenth century, was destined to exercise a far-reaching influence on all the vernacular languages of Europe. Introduced into England about 1476 by William Caxton, who had learned the art on the continent, printing made such rapid progress that a scant century later it was observed that manuscript books were seldom to be met with and almost never used. Some idea of the rapidity with which the new process swept forward may be had from the fact that in Europe the number of books printed before the year 1500 reached the surprising figure of 35,000. The majority of these, it is true, were in Latin, whereas it is in the modern languages that the effect of the printing press is chiefly felt. But in England over 20,000 titles in English had appeared by 1640, ranging all the way from mere pamphlets to massive folios. The result was to bring books, which had formerly been the expensive luxury of the few, within the reach of all. More important, however, was the fact, so obvious today, that it was possible to reproduce a book in a thousand copies or a hundred thousand, every one exactly like the other. A powerful force thus existed for promoting a standard uniform language, and the means were now available for spreading that language throughout the territory in which it was understood. (Baugh, *A History of the English Language*)

Summary   Printing from movable type had a far-reaching influence on all European languages. Within a hundred years, manuscript books had become rare, and over 20,000 titles in English had appeared. Books were now within the reach of everyone and could exert a powerful standardizing influence upon the language.

# WRITING A CRITICAL ANALYSIS OF AN ARGUMENT

A **critical analysis** is an examination of how logically an author has argued his or her case. The word *critical* in this case doesn't mean that you should try to find problems with the author's argument. It means that you should consider whether the argument can stand up to close, objective examination. It is a very rare argument that does not contain some flawed logic, omit some relevant information, or have other shortcomings. In writing a critical analysis, your task is to assess the validity of an argument, outline its limits, and explain *why* it does (or doesn't) seem sound, logical, or well supported.

This last point is essential: in a critical analysis, you aren't concerned with *what* someone is arguing but with *how* the person is arguing it. After all, two people could come to the same conclusion by completely different paths. For example, two people might both feel that the death penalty is wrong, but where one might think that it is morally wrong to kill people, the other might think that torture is a more appropriate penalty than death. A critical analysis would examine the reasons and the evidence that lie behind these conclusions in order to assess their validity.

## Where to Start

Because you have to understand what an author is arguing before you can understand how he or she is arguing it, you'll need to read critically. You can find advice on reading critically on page 24.

To write your analysis, you should focus on the following:

■ **The main thesis or argument of the piece.** What is the overall message the author is trying to convey? Does this central point seem valid or plausible? Why or why not?

■ **The supporting arguments.** Do the claims follow logically from and develop key aspects of the main thesis? Are all of the supporting points that seem necessary present, or do you notice some gaps and omissions? Does each claim seem valid and plausible? Why or why not?

■ **The supporting evidence.** What evidence is the author using to back up any claims? Does the supporting evidence seem authoritative and reasonably complete? Why or why not?

■ **The concluding statement.** Does it follow the argument(s) of the piece? Does it introduce new evidence or claims without following up on them?

■ **How the piece is organized.** Why are the arguments made in the order they are? Would it change the validity of the argument if the order were changed? How do the paragraphs work within the structure of the essay? How do the sentences function? Do they all support the topic sentence and the overall argument?

■ **How the author uses words and stylistic choices as part of the argument.** Has the author led the reader to a certain conclusion by using slanted language or has the author used neutral language? Has the author used terms consistently, or does the definition of some words seem unstable or unclear? Has the author tried to make his or her points clearly, or do you notice efforts to distract readers from the main issues under consideration?

Remember to pay attention to basic details, such as when and where the piece was written. Were there events at the time that may have influenced the author's thinking? Were there things that were not known at the time that cause you, a modern reader, to question the validity of the argument now but would not have influenced you when the piece was written?

## Taking Apart the Argument

Use the following questions to examine the validity of the author's argument:

■ What assumptions has the author made about the topic and about you, the reader? Note that making incorrect assumptions in these areas—what is often called starting with faulty premises—makes the logical foundation shaky and can undermine the validity of the entire argument.

■ What evidence has the author used to support his or her thesis? Is the evidence accurate and authoritative? Is there any evidence that the author should have included but didn't? An argument can be logical only if it offers adequate, appropriate supporting evidence.

■ Do you think the author has made an argument that most people would find persuasive? If so, why? If not, what errors did he or she make?

■ When we write, we write from our own perspective or point of view. This is called "bias." What is the author's bias? How do you know? What would be different in the article if the author had a different bias?

■ What is your own bias as a reader? How does who you are influence how you read this piece of writing?

## Writing Your Analysis

When writing your analysis, it is a good idea to include the following:

- **Introduction**
  - What work are you analyzing?
  - Who was it written by?
  - When was it written?
  - What is the subject?
  - What is its take or stand on the subject (that is, its thesis)?

- **Description**
  - Outline and summarize the article, briefly noting the arguments it makes and the ways in which it makes them.
  - Offer some background information about the piece, particularly noting why it seems to have been written.

- **Analysis**
  - Discuss the validity of the arguments made.

- Examine the ways in which they were made.
- Explore any faults in logic or gaps in reasoning.
- Analyze the author's and your own biases.

- **Conclusion**
  - After stating the overall impression the article makes, judge whether or not it was effectively written and logically argued.
  - Explain how it could have been improved.
  - You might want to acknowledge any ways in which you are biased when examining the piece, including differences in knowledge now as compared to when the piece was written.

Note that these are pieces that should be included in your analysis—some pieces might take up a paragraph, others several paragraphs.

## WRITING A RHETORICAL ANALYSIS

A **rhetorical analysis** thoroughly examines how a piece of writing, or text, does what it does: what is the author's purpose and what techniques or strategies does the author use to achieve that purpose?

Before you begin a rhetorical analysis, it is important that you understand what *rhetoric* is. While the term has a number of definitions, in the context of academic writing it broadly means the use of language to persuade, influence, or communicate. A rhetorical analysis, therefore, examines *how* an author has used language to craft an argument or message in ways that will affect a particular audience.

Check your assignment instructions before you begin to make sure that you know exactly what you are being asked to do. Keep in mind that a rhetorical analysis, unlike a critical analysis, does not ask you to respond to or judge the author's argument. Instead, it asks you to examine the rhetorical choices the author has made and to evaluate whether these make the argument more or less effective.

### Choosing a Text or Texts

Typical rhetorical analysis assignments ask you to analyze a single piece of writing or to compare two or more pieces of writing. You may be given the texts for the assignment or be asked to locate your own texts. If you are responsible for choosing your texts, use the following tips:

■ Narrow your choices as quickly as possible so that you don't waste time finding the right texts that you could better spend working on your analysis.

■ If possible, pick a topic that interests you or that you are familiar with so that you can pay close attention to the text itself rather than the content.

■ Look for pieces that feature a strong argument or point of view. Informational writing, including reports, makes less obvious use of rhetorical devices than do articles meant to communicate a specific argument.

■ Make sure the text you choose is long enough to include sufficient evidence on which to base your observations.

■ If you are comparing two or more articles, choose texts that have very different audiences so that contrasts will be easier to identify.

### Reading Actively and Critically

A good rhetorical analysis is the product of active, critical reading. You will have to read your text or texts repeatedly in order to do a thorough analysis.

• Use your first reading to get a general sense of the text and to familiarize yourself with its parts.

• Starting with your second reading, highlight and take notes to keep track of your observations.

• For suggestions on reading, review "Reading Academic Writing" on page 22.

## Identifying the Rhetorical Situation

Before you begin to analyze the author's rhetorical choices, be sure you understand the context, or *rhetorical situation*, in which the text occurs. Use the following questions to help your reading:

■ **What is the topic?** Once you have a clear idea of the topic, consider the way the topic is treated. Does the text present a specific aspect of the topic? How broadly or narrowly is it examined? Is the topic noteworthy for some reason?

■ **What is the purpose?** Every text has a rhetorical purpose—usually, to inform, to persuade, or to explain. A text's specific purpose might be to entertain, to motivate, or to anger. Many texts have more than one purpose.

■ **What is the thesis, or main point?** What is the author trying to say about the topic? What is the author's position on the key questions raised about the topic? Answering these questions can help you determine the thesis, even if it isn't explicitly stated in a single sentence at the end of the first paragraph. To check your understanding of the thesis, try to summarize it in a sentence or two.

■ **Who is the audience?** Who is the intended reader of the text? What characteristics of the audience might influence the author's argument or choices? Intended readers may be easy to identify, or you may have to infer who they are by analyzing the topic, tone, and specific content of the piece.

## Identifying Rhetorical Strategies

Once you have considered the rhetorical situation, your next step is to examine the author's choices, or rhetorical strategies.

**Look at the structure and form of the text.** How has the author chosen to develop his or her ideas (narrative, explanation, description, comparison, examples, or other methods of development)? How is the text arranged (general to specific, chronological, classification, other pattern)?

**Consider the author's language choices.** These range from paragraph length, sentence structure, and overall organization to the choice of words, the use of transitions, and the way the text looks on the page. They also include the use of figures of speech, imagery, symbolism, repetition, humour, and other devices. Try to identify every feature of the writing that might influence a reader.

**Identify the author's use of persuasive appeals.** If your assignment requires you to analyze how effectively the author has employed *pathos, ethos, and logos,* be sure you understand how each of these persuasive appeals is defined. Then analyze how the author's use of each is revealed through the features of the text. Here are basic definitions of these terms:

■ **Pathos** is using writing to evoke sympathy or empathy. It appeals to people's emotions in order to persuade. Pathetic appeals (appeals to *pathos*) might arouse clear, strong emotions like anger or sorrow or more subtle feelings like sympathy, empathy, or a sense of belonging.

■ **Ethos** is using the fundamental beliefs, feelings, or morals of a time, a movement, a culture, or a group of people to convince an audience that the argument should be believed. Often, ethical appeals (appeals to *ethos*) are concerned with the character of the person who has created the argument. Explicitly describing the numerous academic degrees earned by the author of a newspaper editorial will be persuasive for audiences that value formal education. Word choices and style can make more subtle, implicit ethical appeals. For instance, advertising something as "green" in today's world can make environmentally conscious consumers believe a company shares their morals and thus that its product is a good one to buy. A campaign speech can include contemporary slang that violates the rules of formal grammar in order to make a politician sound friendly and likable to younger voters.

■ **Logos** is the use of logic, reason, and hard facts, such as statistics and examples, to persuade. Logical appeals (appeals to *logos*) are usually emphasized in academic writing, but the other two appeals will often be present in subtle ways.

## Writing the Rhetorical Analysis

**Structure your findings.** First, group your notes into topics that reflect the types of strategies you plan to write about. Try to end up with three or four main subtopics. If you are writing about a single piece of text, your analysis will be organized by those subtopics. If you are comparing texts, you can either deal with your observations about one text and then the next, or you can organize your analysis by subtopic, comparing how the author of each text used certain features.

**Support your assertions.** Be sure to use examples from the text(s) as evidence to back up any statements you make. Be specific and direct in assessing how effective rhetorical strategies, such as persuasive appeals, will be for the intended audience. Explain what you think would be the effects of particular examples on readers and why you think the examples would have those effects.

**Review the guidelines for writing an essay.** Your rhetorical analysis should be structured as an essay, with an introduction, a clear thesis statement, a well-developed body, and a strong conclusion. If you are struggling with how to put your ideas together, review "Writing an Essay" on page 84.

# WRITING A RESEARCH PAPER

Writing a research paper is an excellent opportunity to explore a topic in depth. The research paper is assigned in many disciplines and takes many forms, but underlying them all is the same purpose: to analyze and present your findings on a particular research question.

The research process and guidelines for researching effectively are presented in "Researching" on page 29. The following advice focuses on the process of planning, writing, and editing your research paper.

When you write a research paper, you take the information you have gathered and present it to a reader in a cohesive, clear manner. Often, the paper will argue something, such as why one type of fertilizer is better than another; you will use the information you have gathered to support your point of view, explaining what makes it a better fertilizer.

In order to write an effective research paper, follow the step-by-step process outlined below.

## Choose a Topic

Choosing a topic can be the hardest part of an assignment. You will want your topic to be very specific. This will help you to avoid generalizing. A specific topic also produces a more focused and detailed paper. However, you can begin the research and writing process even if you have only a general idea of the topic. For information on how best to develop a research topic, see page 29.

## Ask Questions and Gather Answers

Once you have chosen a topic, how do you research it? Ask questions.

By making a list of research questions related to your topic, you will not only make it easier to search for information (the answers to your questions) but will also make it easier to formulate a thesis. You can organize your research (facts, figures, quotations, and so forth) by the questions each piece of information answers. For more information on developing good research questions, see page 30.

## Develop a Thesis Statement

A **thesis statement** is one sentence that encapsulates your point of view on the topic. It should be specific and take a stance on the research. At this stage you need only a *working* thesis statement. This means you can adjust the actual statement later. For more information on how to write an effective thesis statement, see page 82.

## Organize

Once you've gathered information, decided how you feel about it, and taken a stand (that is, developed a thesis or argument), you need to organize the ideas you have and the information you have collected. You can do this by creating a mind map or outline. See page 16 for more information.

You will need to decide what point or topic you will address first. Your argument will be most effective if you organize it so that each point leads to the next. Continue until you have written a list of what points you will cover and the order you will cover them in. Your points can come from the questions you asked when researching. For example, you may have asked, "What are the common types of organic or natural fertilizers? What are the benefits of each? What are the negative effects of each? Do they work best alone, or are they more effective when mixed or alternated with other fertilizers?" If you did, you can organize your information by fertilizer type, and further organize it by pros and cons and by most effective usage (that is, alone, mixed with another, or alternated with another).

You will also need to decide what supporting evidence to use for that point or topic. List the facts, data, and quotations you feel support each point in your paper beneath or beside that point. This step will help you see if you have a sufficient number of citations for each point you are making. You may need to do some more research for some sections or cut information from others.

Be sure to include any arguments and evidence that counter your working thesis statement. Rather than ignore what does not agree with your main argument or description, address it. Discuss why you still think what you think or why you support a certain stance, even though an argument or piece of evidence seems to refute it.

## Write

Once you have organized your points and information, you should have a clear idea of what your paper is going to explain to the reader and be able to start writing.

### Body

Start by writing the body of the paper. Explain each point that you want to make in detail and include all supporting evidence. Try to remain within the word count while you are writing. It is time-consuming and difficult to cut words from your draft.

### Introduction and Conclusion

Once you have written the body of the paper, you will have a clear idea of how to introduce it and how to end it. Keep in mind that you need to highlight the context of the research and why it is important for the reader to know and remember what you are explaining in the body of your paper.

In your introduction, you should briefly review existing research in the field in which you are writing, introduce what you are saying (with your thesis statement), and explain what contribution your work will make. You can also state what you will be discussing in more detail later in your essay. In your conclusion, you should summarize the main points of your argument and, once again, explain why you believe what you do and the purpose of the information you have presented.

## Review

Revise your paper once you have a complete first draft. Revisit your working thesis statement. Are you satisfied with the wording? Could you make your argument clearer? Could it better illustrate the points you are making? You may feel you need to tinker with your thesis so that it does, in fact, accurately reflect what you have developed in the body of your essay.

Ensure that each paragraph of the essay contributes to the overall argument. Make changes to the organization and structure if you feel that the paragraph order affects the strength of your argument. Check through all of your supporting evidence to ensure that there are no gaps in your argument, that every piece of information and every topic sentence clearly relates to your thesis, and that you have addressed any concerns or questions readers may have.

When you are satisfied with the thesis statement, organization, and structure, read your sentences aloud. Are they too long? Have you used too many adjectives? Does the order of the sentences in each paragraph make the most sense? Are there any spelling errors? Are there any misplaced modifiers? Have you used a comma where you should have used a period or semicolon?

# WRITING A REPORT

A **report** is a formal document that articulates ideas, conveys research results, or presents factual information in an extended, organized, clear, and detailed way. Reports are used in every profession, from engineering to education, and increasingly in academic courses related to the professions.

Reports are used for many purposes, and as a result, there are many kinds of reports. Among the most common are progress reports, annual reports, research reports, feasibility studies, and financial reports. All have different formats and styles, so be sure you know what kind of report you are being asked to write and then research the expected format and style of that type of report.

The following general guidelines apply to most reports. If you are writing a research report, review the guidelines in "Writing a Research Paper" on page 101. For detailed guidance on how to plan, draft, and revise your writing, review "The Academic Writing Process: 40/20/40" on page 14.

## Planning Your Report

The most important stage in planning a report is determining the purpose and audience for your report. As part of the planning, ask yourself the following questions:

- What is the purpose of my report?
- What key question or questions is my report intended to answer? What problem is it meant to investigate or solve?
- Who will be reading it and why?
- Will my report have more than one audience? If so, which is my primary audience? What considerations does my secondary audience require?
- What information is my report intended to convey?

## Parts of a Report

Reports usually consist of three main parts: the front matter, the body, and the back matter.

### Front Matter

The front matter, which is usually paginated in lower-case roman numerals (iii, v), usually appears in this order:

1. title page, with no page number
2. acknowledgements page, thanking those people who helped you (optional)
3. copy of the letter or memo of authorization, if applicable
4. letter of transmittal
5. table of contents
6. abstract (about 200 words) or executive summary (about 300 words). These are overviews of the report and include a summary of its findings, the analysis of its findings, and conclusions.

7. list of illustrations or list of figures and tables

8. glossary of special terms, key words, and abbreviations used within the report

## Body

The body is the largest section of a report and should contain all the detailed information you are reporting. The sections within the body are organized according to the main topics your report covers.

The pages within the body of your report are numbered using Arabic numerals (1, 2, 3).

The body should include the following parts:

### Introduction

The function of the introduction is to brief your reader about the purpose of the report, the problem it explores, and how you have approached it. It should give the reader sufficient information to read the rest of the report. The introduction typically includes some or all of the following:

- the topic, hypothesis, or research question
- the context of or background to the problem, research, or subject
- a literature review, if appropriate; a statement of the problem to be addressed
- the time frame, telling the reader when the report was initiated and when the research was done
- a list of participants, including their names and skills
- the methodology used in the study (also often presented as a separate section)
- the framework used for the interpretation of the research, including data, a literature review, a summation of previous reports and research, and so forth
- a brief outline of how the report is organized

### Discussion

The main body of the report, sometimes referred to as the discussion, is where you present, analyze, and interpret the information you have gathered. This section must provide the evidence for any conclusions you have drawn or recommendations you have made, including

- descriptions
- qualitative and quantitative data
- arguments, with explanations and analyses

Use subheadings to divide the discussion into the main points or subtopics and ensure that the topics are arranged logically. Organize each section so that the main point is presented first, followed by the supporting evidence. You may end each subsection with a short conclusion.

### Conclusion

The conclusion of your report presents your answer to the problem or research question you presented in the introduction. It is where you state your conclusions and, if required, make recommendations based on what you have found or researched. (Note:

In some reports, especially policy reports, recommendations are made in the executive summary or in a separate section after the conclusions.)

### Back Matter

Depending on what sort of report you are writing, you may wish to include back matter, which may include notes, appendices, references, and an index (only in very long reports). If you include appendices, they should support the analyses and explanations in the body of the report; they may include technical definitions and explanations, series of graphs and tables, and survey results. Appendices should be cross-referenced at the appropriate place in the body of the report; if you cannot find a place to add a cross-reference, it is a good indication that the appendix is not relevant to the report.

The references or bibliography section lists all reading you referred to in order to prepare for and write the report, formatted according to the documentation style you are using. Refer to "Documentation Styles" on page 48 for details.

## Writing Your Report

Reports are often read by many people, and each will be looking for specific information. Think of your report as a piece of writing that allows readers to quickly scan and easily understand the information most relevant to them.

Plan, draft, and revise your report as you would any other assignment. For help with the stages of writing a report, review "The Academic Writing Process: 40/20/40" on page 14 for general guidelines.

## Report-Writing Tips

■ Write the body of your report before you write your abstract/executive summary. It is easiest to summarize what has already been written.

■ Write in clear, simple, focused sentences. The content of your writing may be complex and highly specialized, so the actual form of your writing has to be plain and simple. Your report should be easily read by anyone who may read it.

■ Check the coherence of your report. Outline your report in as much detail as possible, even down to the paragraph level, before you begin writing. Use the introduction to the report and introductions to the main subsections to say what each presents as a way to keep your report from wandering.

■ Check that everything you include in your report is relevant to the purpose and the audience. It can be tempting once you have gathered evidence to use it, even if it does not contribute to the purpose of your report. If it doesn't contribute to the answers you are looking for, throw it out.

■ Define all terminology. Avoid jargon (industry-specific language) without first defining it or including it in your glossary. Even if you are writing for specialists, consider whether non-specialists are also part of your audience.

■ Make your report visually appealing. Use headings and subheadings to help your reader scan through the report to find the information relevant to them. Use graphs to illustrate results. Use tables to organize figures.

## Types of Reports

### Co-op Work-Term Reports

Your work-term report is aimed at several audiences: your work supervisor, other students, and the co-op coordinator. It is best to write it formally, although you may write it as a personal essay. It should include

- a thesis or proposition
- a one-page executive summary
- a table of contents
- a list of the people included in your report, including
  - their names
  - their qualifications
  - any other relevant information
- background to the report, including
  - information about the position
  - information about your studies at university
  - information about your employer
- information about
  - what you learned
  - how you applied skills gained at university to your work experience
  - how you benefitted from your work experience
  - any problems you experienced (and how you overcame them, if applicable)
  - how your work met or did not meet your expectations
  - examples of how you completed the tasks assigned to you
- any explanations or analyses you feel are necessary
- a conclusion based on the description of the facts and your experience

### Proposals

A project or business proposal should aim to give potential sponsors or employers information about the project and its feasibility. A good proposal includes the following:

- information and background, including what the project is
- the purpose and objective of the project, detailing
  - why you want to do the project
  - who it will benefit
  - how it will benefit them
  - how it will benefit the potential sponsor(s)/employer(s)
- the scope of the project (how far it reaches)
- possible ways in which the project can be executed, including information about
  - how you plan to complete the project
  - a simpler option and a more expansive option
  - ways in which the project could be expanded if it is successful
  - how it relates to previous research/businesses

- how it will benefit or impact future developments
- why it is reasonable and feasible
- who will be involved

- a detailed timeline
- the cost/budget, details about where you plan to get the money, and an estimate of when it will start to make money (if applicable)
- analyses of any complications or problems that could impact the project and details of how you would overcome them, including financial backup
- a conclusion or overall pitch that highlights the benefits of undertaking the project

## Progress Reports

Progress reports are intended to inform a person or organization about the current standing of a project. An example of a progress report is a school report card, which details to parents and students the students' current standing in the subjects they are studying and how they can improve. Progress reports usually include

- an introduction or background, detailing the overall project
- a description of the current standing of the project, including
  - how much of the work is complete
  - how much of the work remains to be done
  - where the project stands in terms of time estimates (that is, is the project on schedule, ahead of schedule, or behind schedule?)
  - any complications that have occurred, including how they were overcome or whether they are still a problem
- new estimates of timeline and cost, if needed
- details of what will be completed between the time of the current report and the next progress report
- a conclusion

## Financial Reports

Financial reports are common in the business world. They are often submitted on a quarterly basis to inform executives, company owners, shareholders, and customers of the current financial standing of a company. They usually include

- an introduction discussing the company background and its current projects, completed projects, upcoming projects, and goals for the future
- a description of the current financial standing of the company (a balanced budget), detailing the current assets and liabilities of the company
- a description of the profits and losses of the company, including current income and expenses
- a description of any changes to the base holdings of a company
- a description of the movement of company money (cash flows), including a discussion of investment earnings and banking activities
- a summary or conclusion, stating overall gains or losses and, possibly, projections for the coming quarter

# WRITING A LAB REPORT

When you write a **lab report**, you demonstrate your grasp of the premise of the lab, show your processes in completing the lab, and present the conclusions you have reached based upon the data you gathered during the lab. The lab report has a standard structure that you must follow when presenting this information.

Please refer to your lab manual for specific instructions on writing a lab report and details about faculty-specific reports. (That is, a report for chemistry will differ in some ways from a report for biology or physics. Please refer to your lab manual to ensure that you are handing in a report as specified by the department.)

## Abstract

Although this section appears first in your report, it should be written last. It outlines your purpose, your findings, your conclusions, and the significance of your conclusions. You should dedicate one or two sentences to each of these points, so your report should be roughly four to eight sentences in length, or one hundred to two hundred words.

## Introduction/Objective

This section of the report explains, in more detail, the purpose of your experiment. It should also give any background information necessary for the reader to understand the experiment, such as relevant theories and equations. More detailed reports will also discuss previous research in the area. If you are including a detailed explanation of theories or previous research, consider adding a section dedicated to theory, background, or research (see below).

## Theory/Background

The theory or background section is an optional section usually reserved for in-depth discussions of any theories behind your experiment and any previous research requiring discussion.

## Apparatus List

Not all labs require you to outline the materials and apparatus used, but some do. You may report the materials and apparatus you use in list form. If you are using chemicals as part of your lab, record any hazards beside the chemicals in use. (For example, if you were to list HCl, hydrochloric acid, as a material being used, you should write next to it that it is corrosive and can damage tissue if strong enough.)

## Procedure

In this section, you describe the experiment in detail. It should be completed in chronological order and is best presented in list form. For each step, describe exactly what you did. If you deviated from the desired process, say so.

## Data

Write down all measurements. If there was some uncertainty about the result, note it next to the measurement. (For example, *NaCl concentration = 1.65M—theoretical; wind blew some granules; therefore concentration must be slightly lower than 1.65M in practice*.) Include all variations, deviations, and uncertainties in this section as well. (For example, *NaCl concentration = 1.65M ± .02M*)

You will usually hand in a copy of your in-lab notes at the end of an experiment so that your TA can cross-reference your results if the TA believes you are reporting false or altered data. Despite this, you must still list your data in your formal report. It is best if it is typed and organized into tables, lists, or charts where possible.

### Calculations/Results

Record any equations or calculations you do clearly, showing all steps and units. Any graphs or charts that accompany this section should be referred to in the main report and attached to the back of your typewritten report. Anything hand-written should be written in pen and be legible, clear, and concise.

### Discussion

The discussion is the most important part of the lab report. You should spend more time writing it than any other part of the report, and be sure to provide all details. Refer back to your experimental objective when you discuss the lab: did your lab fulfill the objective? Why or why not?

Your discussion should

- summarize how your experiment fulfilled or did not fulfill the lab objectives
- state what occurred during the lab
- report any errors
- summarize and analyze the results of your experiment
- explain any possible errors and deviation
- explain why your results were flawed if they were flawed
- explain why your results were not what you expected if they were not what you expected
- discuss the inclusion of any tables, charts, or graphs and their significance
- discuss any difference between experimental and theoretical values and the significance of such differences
- discuss anything you aren't sure about
- refer to any laws or theories being tested and discuss whether your results confirm or deny those laws or theories and why

If necessary or beneficial, you can also compare your results to those of others and discuss why your results varied. Be sure to include the reports of those whose results you discuss in your references.

If your results were flawed to the point where you cannot base a conclusion on them and you have received permission from your instructor or TA to use a colleague's results to reach a conclusion, mention the fact here and then complete the discussion as listed above using the results you have been allowed to borrow. However, do not forget to include a discussion of why your results were flawed and what you learned from your own results. Be sure to include the reports of those whose results you discuss in your references.

## Conclusion

The conclusion should be very short (one or two sentences). It should sum up what you learned in the lab and include observational evidence. If you could make your objective into a question, the conclusion would be the answer. For example, if your objective was to discover whether the reaction between chemicals F and G is endothermic, your conclusion would state, "As the temperature of the solution rose from X degrees Celsius to Y degrees Celsius when chemical Z was added, the reaction between F and G is exothermic, not endothermic."

## References

List any sources you have used. Include

- your lab manual
- any lab reports or results other than your own that you discussed or used
- any other experiments or reports you discussed
- any sources of included background information (websites, books, others)

## Appendices

Any graphs, tables, notes, readings, or other additional material included in your lab should be listed under the "Appendices" heading. (For example, *Appendix A: Graph of temperatures at ten second intervals throughout reaction.*)

# PREPARING A CLOSE READING

A **close reading** is a detailed analysis of a short passage of text, usually taken from a larger work. It is used in the study of literature to demonstrate something specific that is based upon small details, such as a text's use of diction, punctuation, or figurative language.

Close readings are assigned to make you pay attention to small details. They will help you to practise analytical skills and to learn how details—diction, punctuation, repetition, figurative language—work in texts to demonstrate both small matters of importance and overarching themes. You can think of a close reading as a section of an essay—a single paragraph or group of paragraphs (depending on the specifics of your assignment) that argues a part of an overall thesis.

## What to Include

As with an essay, a close reading assignment should have an argument or main point that you are trying to prove. In a close reading, you could argue, for example, that a text's use of rarely used, mellifluous words enhances the description of an aristocratic family as extravagant traditionalists. You could argue that the way characters' speech is broken by punctuation exemplifies their fear. Your close reading should show precisely how the words of the text you are analyzing support your argument, and it should broaden the picture by placing the passage or section you analyze in context.

It is a good idea to focus on what a single word or phrase accomplishes, especially if it is repeated or emphasized in some way. You should be able to write a paragraph on a single word if you ask yourself what it means, what it means in the context of the piece, whether it is being used ironically or is alluding to something more than its basic meaning, how and why it has been used, where it is placed and why, what surrounds it and why, how it links parts of the piece or sentence together, and what all this achieves—in the context of the piece.

## What to Look For

When you are doing a close reading of a short passage, there are many things you can examine to pick out threads and themes. You should keep in mind the overall work, not just your chosen or assigned passage when doing this. Remember, the best close readings relate the way language is used within the passage to the overall themes of the work.

Here are some things you should pay attention to:

- diction (word choice)
- punctuation
- repetition of words
- repetition of grammatical structures
- figurative language (simile, metaphor, and others)
- allusion
- imagery and description
- sentence structure and grammar

- voice
- use of sounds (alliteration, consonance, assonance, dissonance)
- point of view
- nuance (irony, euphemism, sarcasm)
- style

## The Close Reading Process

Make a copy of the passage (photocopy or printout) and annotate it (highlight, circle, write notes, and so on), paying attention to the elements listed above and noting anything else important. Pick out important elements, such as setting and character. Place the passage within the text, if you can. When does it occur? What is happening in the plot at that point? What sort of feelings or thoughts is the text trying to elicit? When you have done all this, pick out the most interesting observations—and the ones that will make the most coherent analysis—and write up your close reading.

As with any essay, your close reading should include an introduction (with a thesis), a body with three or more main points, and a conclusion. For further details, see "Writing an Essay" on page 84.

Look at the example below to get an idea of how a close reading works.

> Elizabeth Barrett Browning's "Sonnet XLIII" productively uses the tension between what is quantifiable—"Let me count" (1)—and what is abstract—for example, "Being and ideal Grace" (4)—to show how difficult it is to communicate how it feels to be in love. In line 7, for example, the word "freely," when it describes how the speaker loves, suggests a spontaneous and voluntary response to the lover who is the addressee of the sonnet. When the word is also attached to how "men strive for Right," however, it suggests struggle and conflict, an active attempt to achieve a difficult goal. By using the same adverb ("freely") in application to two verbs ("love" and "strive"), Barrett Browning questions whether and how striving for right and the act of love are comparable. The idea that mankind's urge for "Right" is a free one is not universal; it depends on the definition of abstract terms. (What is it to be free? What is right?) But the problem of defining words like "love," "free," and "right"—terms that are subjective and mutable—is exactly the problem of a poem that endeavors to explain how love works: "How do I love thee?" (1) Line 7 betrays the poet's awareness that the explanation is inevitably subjective. Until this point in the poem, she has used vocabulary of measurement and boundary to attempt concrete and quantifiable descriptions: line 2, for instance, imagines measurements of the soul's "depth and breadth and height." This line, however, marks a surrender to abstract terms and, eventually, to the unknowable workings of God's choices and of life "after death" (13–14).

# PREPARING A PRESENTATION

No matter how experienced or inexperienced you are as a presenter, or how relaxed or nervous you are about speaking to a roomful of people, careful preparation will make it much more likely that your presentation will be a success.

People who "wing it" may look enviably relaxed, but they often give terrible presentations. Unprepared speakers often fail to fill the time they are given or go overtime. They repeat themselves and leave out facts. They don't support their arguments properly. They aren't clear.

In addition to the ideas below, think about presentations you enjoyed and ones you found uninteresting or unclear. What features made the good ones better than the others?

## Developing Your Presentation

### Gather Your Information

Before you do anything else, gather the information you need on the topic. If you are going to need detailed information on the hygienic practices of the court of Elizabeth I and you know nothing about hygiene in sixteenth-century England, you won't be able to give a good presentation.

For tips on researching effectively, refer to "Researching" on page 29.

### Identify Your Purpose and Audience

Why are you making this presentation? Who is it for? These are the two most important questions you can ask yourself when preparing to present. Explaining cortical-spreading depression to a room full of neurochemists will be very different from explaining it to a group of people who suffer from migraines and work in various professions. You need to consider the following:

- What the audience knows and what they may not know
  - What do you need to explain?
  - What do they already understand?
  - How can you make concepts they are unfamiliar with easy for them to understand?
- Why the audience is there
  - What information are they hoping to get out of your presentation?
  - What information do you want them to get out of the presentation?
  - Why are you giving the presentation? For a class? For a conference?
- How you present your information
  - How will you frame or contextualize it?
  - How will you get from one section to another?
  - How will you make a complex process seem simple and straightforward?

From the answers to these questions, you should be able to develop an outline of your presentation—what information you need to fit in and what you will have to cut, and what questions you should address.

## Outline

Once you know what you want to say and how you want to say it, you can start to arrange it. Consider how to introduce your topic. How can you make the topic seem interesting—or convey how interesting it is—to your audience? What do they need or want to know?

Start to arrange your information as you would in an essay. Create an introduction. Separate your information into topics and subtopics. Brainstorm ways to finish effectively. Organize your material into a logical sequence.

## Create Supporting Materials

**Decide what you will use.** If you are planning to include visuals in your presentation, decide what and how beforehand. Are you going to create a slide show? Are you going to make a poster or flipchart? Will you use an overhead projector?

The most important thing to remember if you are planning to use supporting materials is this: they are *supporting materials*. What you say and how you say it should be the main part of your presentation. You should not read from charts or slides, and your audiovisuals should not detract or distract from what you are saying.

**Consider possible problems.** Will your flipchart be visible from the back of the room? Will you need to arrange for a microphone? Will your software be compatible with the computers available, or should you bring your own? Will your computer work with the available projectors?

One of the most distracting problems during a presentation is when supporting materials don't work as they should. To avoid this, take your supporting materials for a test drive. If you are able, go to the room in which you will be presenting to do this. Make sure all of your cords work properly, that you have a way to stick that poster to the board. Problems you haven't thought of will make themselves evident when you practise.

**Prepare for the worst.** Always have a backup plan. What will you do if it rains on your flipchart or someone spills tea on your laptop? Do you have your presentation saved in your email inbox? Remember Murphy's Law: if it can go wrong, it will. Make sure that you can still present if it does.

## Practise

You've heard it a million times before and will probably hear it again. One of the reasons this little cliché exists is its truth. Practise does make perfect—or at least near perfect. If you've gone through your presentation ten times on your own, you won't feel so worried about it going wrong when you do it for real.

The other great thing about practising is that you can troubleshoot. Is your presentation long enough? Is it too long? Have you left yourself time to answer questions from the audience? Is a certain phrase hard to say? Do you need a clicker to change between slides? Problems you didn't think of before will become evident as you walk through your presentation.

You will also be able to hear what you've written being said aloud. Does it sound good, or is it a little flat? Is it engaging? You can tweak your presentation to make it better if you give yourself time to practise.

## Engaging Your Audience

Your actual presentation will have more impact and will be more engaging if you build in some of the following techniques:

### Use Repetition

Good speakers often use repetition so that the audience can remember the most important information. Repeating information can also help you remind yourself, when you are nervous, about what you've said and what you have left to say.

A great way to start a presentation is by telling the audience what you are going to tell them: "Today, I am going to tell you how to make a great presentation. To do this, I will go over preparation, presentation, and some calming techniques you can use." This not only tells the audience what to expect, but also allows you to let them know where you are in your presentation and precisely what you are telling them: "I just told you five things that are important in preparing for a presentation: research, considering your purpose and audience, outlining, supporting material, and practice. Now I am going to tell you some techniques you can use to make your presentation great!"

### Use Questions

There are two types of questions you can use in a presentation: rhetorical questions, or questions you don't actually expect an answer to (such as, "How could he have thought setting fire to his pants was a good idea?"), and actual questions.

Rhetorical questions invite the audience to remain focused on what you are saying. They can often add humour to a presentation, as well.

Real questions engage the audience in your presentation. If you allow your listeners to feel as though they are part of the presentation, you will keep them focused—and, as an added bonus, you will remind yourself that they, too, are human, which makes them seem much less scary.

Audience participation keeps presentations engaging. Asking questions, eliciting ideas, and requesting examples from the audience will help people feel involved and important. You may be able to create some questions to offer as a guided discussion activity either at the end of or intermittently throughout your presentation.

If you are going to take questions at the end of your presentation, try to predict the kinds of questions you will be asked. Thinking of an answer while you are standing up in front of people can be daunting, but if you have predicted questions and developed answers ahead of time, you will be more prepared and more relaxed.

### Use Visuals

Another way to engage your audience is the strategic use of visuals. Visuals can include pictures, signs, PowerPoint slides, or words on the white board. Key words should be highlighted with visuals, as should important names or words that the audience might have trouble understanding.

Visuals are an effective way of emphasizing a point. Telling people that a great white shark is powerful is one thing; telling them and then showing them footage of a great white propelling itself out of the water and swallowing a fur seal whole is another.

There are some things you should be aware of when using visuals (especially computer slides):

- Pay attention to sizes, fonts, and colour. Will the audience be able to read the information easily, or will it be hard for them to see that yellow, swirly font on a red background?

- Your visuals shouldn't distract from *you*. Your speech—not your visuals—is the main part of the presentation.

- Remember to keep visuals appropriate for the audience. Two-year-olds might not want to see the great white shark eat the cute seal.

- Don't let animations, gimmicky slide transitions, or goofy clip-art distract people from the message.

- Pay attention to how long your visuals take (especially if using animation). Most presentation software includes a practice-timing feature. Use it so you know exactly how long your presentation will take.

- Don't rely too heavily on visuals or read from your slides/posters/charts.

- Don't crowd your slides with too much information or too many visuals.

- Proofread your slides. Mistakes detract and distract.

- Practise your presentation with your slideshow to be sure you know how the two will go together.

## Speaking Well

Some people seem to have a natural ability to speak well. If you analyze what they do, you will find common elements, some of which are listed below.

### Pace Yourself

Good speakers take their time. People often speed up their speech when they are nervous: don't let yourself. Tell yourself that you have plenty of time. Focus on saying your information clearly. Practise speaking slowly and leaving pauses between points so you don't sound rushed.

### Enunciate

Pay attention to making each word heard. Focus on *d*'s, *t*'s, *p*'s, and *b*'s, which are often lost or slurred. Is it "don'*d*" or "don'*t*"? Make sure you speak clearly.

### Stay Composed

Don't rock back and forth, pace restlessly, wiggle your foot, chew your lip, or fidget with your shirt cuff. These are all very distracting. Stand or walk in a relaxed manner. Use natural gestures so that you look like a human and not like a mannequin.

### Make Sure Your Audience Can Hear You

Focus on pushing your air from your diaphragm (your stomach). Aim to have your voice heard right to the back of the room. Your regular speaking voice may be too quiet to be heard except in the front row, so practise notching up the volume when preparing to speak in public.

### Repeat Questions

If you are asked a question, repeat it so that everyone in the audience can hear it. If you answer a question nobody else heard, they will want to know what your answer means.

### Pause

Pauses emphasize what you are saying and make you seem important. Silence draws people's attention. Don't fill empty spaces with *um's* and *er's*. Pauses also allow people to catch up with what you've said. This is important, especially if the topic is noe or unfamiliar to them.

### Appear Confident

You don't have to be confident, but you want to *appear* confident. Try to stay relaxed and composed, even if you feel your hands shake. If you appear confident, your audience will think you are confident—and you will feel more confident if you act it.

### Maintain Eye Contact

Look at your audience. Make eye contact with individuals, hold their eyes for a few seconds, and then move on. If you can't look *at* people, look *near* them. Talk to the armrest of the chair of someone in the back row or a spot on the wall.

### Smile

Even the slightest curve of your lips will help to put both yourself and your audience at ease. Try to seem like you are enjoying giving the presentation.

### Speak, Don't Read

Don't read from your paper. Make cue cards so that you can keep track of where you are in your speech, look down at them, and then *look up* and speak.

## Tips for the Nervous Speaker

There are many techniques you can use to calm yourself down before a presentation, even if you haven't prepared and practised (which you should). Here are some great ones.

### Take a Deep Breath

It seems a cliché, but it truly works. If you are panicking, slowing your breathing, breathing in through your nose and out through your mouth, and holding deep breaths in your lungs for a few seconds before letting them out can really help to calm you.

### Listen to Music

Music can calm you down or distract you from what feels like impending doom. Go ahead and listen to it while you set up your space or between the presentations that precede your own.

### Do Something Fun

Watch a film, play a game, get coffee with a friend—do anything that will make you laugh and distract you. It will help take your mind off your worries about public speaking.

### Move

Take the dog for a walk, do some chores, stretch, or go for a long run. Moving can help shake out your need to fidget and can help you relax.

### Visualize

Think of a safe place, a person you love, a good memory, your favourite meal, or an event you are looking forward to. Happy thoughts make happy presenters.

### Pretend

Pretend that you actually enjoy standing in front of a group of other people and speaking. Pretend that you are a world-famous presenter and that people have flocked from all across the country just to hear what you have to say. Pretend that you are someone else. If you pretend hard enough, you might just get through your presentation without panicking.

# PREPARING FOR AN EXAM

Exams can be nerve-wracking. But you are less likely to feel less anxious and more likely to do well if you have prepared yourself as thoroughly as possible. Remember to start early and allow yourself enough time to go through all the following steps.

## Before Exam Day

### Get Organized

Ask your instructor what the exam is likely to include and then gather your course outline, class notes, previous assignments, and tests so that you are ready to organize your study notes. Go back to your course outline to review the course goals and objectives. In gathering your study material, focus on information that will help you demonstrate that you have understood the main course concepts and are able to apply those concepts to other information, situations, and problems (since this is what your exam is likely to require). Prune out anything that you don't need to review or that your exam is unlikely to test.

### Use Effective Reading and Organizing Strategies

Read for the main ideas presented in course materials. Read actively, annotating and note-taking as you read. (For more active reading strategies, see page 22.) Use graphic organizers (concept maps, charts, tables, diagrams, and others) to sort information in ways that will make it easier for you to remember details and to show how different ideas and concepts connect.

### Anticipate the Exam

Review the course syllabus, assignments, and previous tests to see what questions and what sort of questions were asked. What did the instructor want you to learn in this course? What did you focus on throughout the course? Are there any important parts of the course you haven't yet been tested on? Can you see patterns in the way your instructor asks questions or in what material he or she bases questions on? Make sure you can critically evaluate and analyze subject matter and support that evaluation/analysis by providing evidence.

You can often find old exams for your course or similar courses in the library or elsewhere on campus. Review them to see what kinds of questions were asked.

Think about what you have been studying. If you were the instructor, what kinds of questions would you ask? What topics would you focus on? What would you look for in an answer?

### Practise under Pressure

Think about what kind of questions you will be asked. Develop your own practice questions or exams. Try to answer the questions in a set amount of time without referring to your notes.

It is often a good idea to do this with fellow students, so you can take each other's practice exams. Discuss one another's tests. Has anyone asked something that you didn't think would be asked? Ask the person why he or she asked it? You might discover a potential question that you had overlooked.

## Use Different Approaches to Studying

Making notes and rereading those notes is one way to study. It can also be worthwhile to try different approaches. When you take the knowledge and concepts from the course and apply them, you can determine if there are gaps in your understanding and you can better ensure your comprehension of what you are studying. Here are some other approaches to studying.

■ Try giving a mini-lecture from your notes. Can you talk about the material confidently? What questions might those in the audience ask?

■ Form a study group so you can practise explaining the concepts to each other and develop sample questions to use for exam practice.

■ Watch online videos that include the information. If you are studying the life of Catherine the Great, is there a documentary about her life that you can get online or in the library?

■ Make up a catchy song about what you are studying and record it on your computer. Writing a simple rhyme can help as well.

■ Make a diagram to help you remember relationships and parts of a whole. A concept map (see page 16 for a sample) can demonstrate how DNA mutates or show the elements of String Theory. A timeline can track the development of the Industrial Revolution or outline who studied probability, how, and when.

■ Create examples in which you can apply the knowledge you are acquiring. For example, you can practise applying a mathematical formula in different situations.

■ Make a drama or dialogue that helps you remember important facts. Staging a mock battle between Allied and Axis powers with your friends or creating a dialogue between two important theorists can deepen your understanding of what you are reading about.

## Writing the Exam

### Analyze the Exam Questions

When you first get the exam paper, take time to look through all the questions and sections before you begin. It might be better to start at the back, where the big-point questions are often asked, than at the front with the easy, one-point questions. Get an idea of what you will have to do and budget your time (that is, consider the percentage value in deciding how much time to spend on each section). Make sure you read the instructions and questions carefully. Underline key verbs, such as *define*, *explain*, and *compare and contrast* to help yourself focus on what you have to demonstrate.

Allow yourself time to review your answers, comparing them to the questions. Did you do everything you were asked to do? Could you say anything more on the subject? Have you shown your process, or have you left out steps?

### Planning and Drafting Essay Questions

If your exam includes essay questions, plan your writing before you start. Effective planning at the beginning will help you cut down on drafting and writing time; it will also help to ensure that you answer the question thoroughly and concisely.

Think about how you want to approach the questions and how much time you have to complete each section. Do a brief outline or a mind map on a piece of scrap paper to get your ideas down. Write out any facts or figures you know that relate to the subject. Can you include them in the essay somehow? Where would they best fit?

When writing an exam, be sure to address the "why" and "how" instead of simply answering "what." Support your points with strong evidence and examples. Imagine that your reader knows nothing on the topic except what is common knowledge.

## Writing and Proofreading

Slow down. Take the time to write neatly and legibly. Leave a generous margin and double space your work if you can so you have space to revise or add to your answer.

If you are writing an essay question, leave yourself some time for proofreading. Read your essay backward, paying special attention to spelling and punctuation errors. Then read it forward, checking for the completeness and logic of your argument. Ensure that you have answered the question completely. Make sure there are no factual errors and that all your claims are backed up by evidence.

If you are writing proofs or solutions, make sure that you have shown your process. Also check that you have included all units of measurement. How did you get moles from grams and millilitres? You can lose marks very easily by forgetting to show your logic when writing essays or balancing equations.

# PART III: ACADEMIC WRITING RESOURCES

# English Grammar Basics

A knowledge of English grammar will not by itself make you a good writer, but it can help you understand and identify errors in your writing. The following section defines the terms commonly used to talk about English grammar and provides tips on how to avoid common grammatical errors.

## PARTS OF SPEECH

English has eight parts of speech: *nouns, pronouns, adjectives* (including *articles*), *verbs, adverbs, prepositions, conjunctions,* and *interjections.*

### Nouns

A **noun** refers to a person (*professor, Wilma*), place (*home, UVic*), object (*car, tree*), or abstract quality (*fear, love, revenge*). Nouns are either singular (*book*) or plural (*books*). All nouns are either **proper nouns or common nouns** and either **count nouns** or **non-count** (or **uncountable) nouns.**

**Proper nouns**, such as the name of a person, country, or company, are always capitalized (*Gerald, India, Microsoft*). **Common nouns** are capitalized only at the beginning of a sentence.

**Count nouns** are nouns that can be counted and can form a plural; for example, *cookie/cookies, bicycle/bicycles, goose/geese*).

**Non-count nouns** name things that cannot be numbered and therefore cannot form a plural (*sand, knowledge, weather, copper*).

**Contextual nouns** are nouns that can be either countable or non-countable, depending on their context.

| | |
|---|---|
| Count | I need *a light* in my office (*light* refers to a lamp or light fixture, a countable item). |
| Non-count | Let there be *light* (*light* refers to the presence of light, which is abstract and therefore uncountable). |

Many abstract ideas are uncountable (*love, courage, loneliness, beauty*), but they become countable when they refer to a specific kind.

| | |
|---|---|
| Count | Her new car is a *beauty.* |
| Non-count | *Love* is blind. |

### Pronouns

A **pronoun** takes the place of a noun. A pronoun usually stands in for a specific noun, which is called its **antecedent.**

## Pronouns

| Type | Pronouns | Example |
|------|----------|---------|
| Personal | *I, you, he, she, it, we, you, they, me, you, him, her, it, them* | Corey offered *her* the book, but *she* had already read *it*. |
| Relative | *who, whom, whose, that, which, what, whoever, whomever, whichever, whatever* | Esha has a roommate *who* likes to garden. |
| Indefinite | *all, any, anyone, both, neither, few, none, some,* and many others | Most students completed their work on time, but *some* were late. |
| Demonstrative | *this, that, these, those* | I plan to include *this* in my essay. |
| Interrogative | *what, why, which, whom, who, whose,* and others | *Which* do you prefer, tomatoes or onions? |
| Reflexive | *myself, yourself, himself, herself, itself, ourselves, yourselves, themselves* | The theory *itself* is a problem for researchers. |
| Reciprocal | *each other, one another* | They haven't spoken to *each other* for years. |

The **case** of a pronoun indicates whether the pronoun functions as a subject, an object, or a possessive. Some pronouns change form depending on their case.

| Subjective Case | Objective Case | Possessive Case |
|-----------------|----------------|-----------------|
| *I* | *me* | *my, mine* |
| *you* | *you* | *your, yours* |
| *he* | *him* | *his* |
| *she* | *her* | *her, hers* |
| *it* | *it* | *its* |
| *we* | *us* | *our, ours* |
| *they* | *them* | *their, theirs* |

Example

**Subjective:** *We* wanted to say, "Happy Friday!" [*We* functions as the subject of the sentence.]

**Objective:** They wished *us* a happy Friday. [*Us* functions as the object of *wished.*]

**Possessive:** The problem was *ours*. [*Ours* indicates ownership of *problem*.]

## Adjectives

**Adjectives** modify nouns and pronouns by describing or quantifying them.

Example                    The *busy* chef quickly broiled the *fresh* fish to appease the *loud*, *hungry* campers.

Adjectives have three forms: **positive**, **comparative**, and **superlative**.

Positive                   *small, beautiful, bad*

Comparative                *smaller, more beautiful, worse*

Superlative                *smallest, most beautiful, worst*

Sometimes, you need to use more than one adjective to describe a noun.

**Coordinate adjectives** modify a noun equally. If you can use *and* between the adjectives, they are coordinate. You separate coordinate adjectives with a comma.

Example                    His *convoluted, complex* prose is hard to comprehend.

If the adjective closest to the noun is more related to the noun than the other(s), the adjectives are not coordinate and should not be separated by a comma.

Example                    The *damaged library* books are in the basement.

**Compound adjectives** are two or more words acting together as a single modifier. Often compound adjectives are hyphenated to avoid confusion.

Example                    The *well-written* essay got a good grade.

The hyphen signals *well-written* is an adjective and that both the adverb *well* and the adjective *written* are working together to modify the noun.

### Articles

Articles are the most frequently used adjectives. There are two articles: the **indefinite article,** *a* (*an* before a vowel sound) and the **definite article,** *the*. Articles precede nouns and other adjectives.

The **definite** article (*the*) is used to refer to a specific noun.

Example                    Jazmin climbed *the* tree in the backyard. [Names a specific tree.]

The **indefinite** article (*a, an*) is used to refer to a non-specific noun.

Example                    Jazmin looked for *a* gas station. [Refers to any gas station.]

**Using *a* or *an***

*A* is used before words that begin with a consonant sound (not just a consonant letter).

Example                    Kiera wanted to find *a* <u>u</u>nicorn; it was *a* <u>h</u>ope she'd fostered for years.

*An* is used before words that begin with a vowel sound (not just a vowel letter), including words that begin with a silent *h*.

Example                    The Boy Scout ran from *an* <u>a</u>ngry bear for *an* <u>h</u>our.

Using articles with count and non-count nouns

A count noun does not take an article when it is *plural* and *non-specific*.

Examples                  Asher likes *pies* rather than cakes. [*Pies* is non-specific.]
                          Asher likes *the pies* that are topped with whipped cream.
                          [Refers to specific pies.]

(For suggestions on how to use articles correctly, see page 135.)

## Adverbs

An **adverb** modifies the meaning of a verb, an adjective, another adverb, or a whole sentence.

Example                   *Unfortunately*, the *tornado almost totally destroyed* the *surpris-ingly* pretty town. [*Unfortunately* modifies the whole sentence; *almost* modifies the adverb *totally*; *totally* modifies the verb *destroyed*; *surprisingly* modifies the adjective *pretty*.]

Adverbs appear in three forms:

Positive                  *far, often, quickly*

Comparative               *farther, more often, less quickly*

Superlative               *farthest, most often, least quickly*

## Verbs

**Verbs** express an action (*cough, study, bite*) or a state of being (*seem, be, exist*). Verbs change form depending on whether they describe the present or the past (*give/gave, make/made; do/did*) and when their subject is a singular noun or third-person singular pronoun (*the dog barks; it moves*).

### Verb Tense

**Verb tense** expresses the element of time. There are three main verb tenses: **present**, **past**, and **future**. Each of these also has a **perfect** tense, a **progressive** tense, and a **perfect progressive** tense.

### Transitive, Intransitive, and Linking Verbs

Verbs can be transitive or intransitive (and sometimes both) or linking (copulative).

**Transitive verbs** require an object to complete their meaning. The **direct object** receives the action of the verb.

**Intransitive verbs** do not require an object to complete their meaning. The action remains with the subject.

Transitive                Erica *lifted* the book.

Intransitive              Janpreet *daydreamed*.

The direct object of a transitive verb answers the question, "*What* (or *whom*) received the action of the verb?"

## Present Tense

| Tense | Definition | Example |
|-------|------------|---------|
| Simple Present | indicates action that is occurring or regularly occurs, or states a fact | *She studies every morning.* |
| Present Progressive | indicates action that is happening in the present | *She is studying right now.* |
| Present Perfect | indicates an action that began in the past and is continuing in the present | *She has studied for four hours.* |
| Present Perfect Progressive | indicates an action that began in the past, is occurring in the present, and is likely to continue | *She has been studying since last night.* |

## Past Tense

| Tense | Definition | Example |
|-------|------------|---------|
| Simple Past | indicates an action that was completed in the past | *She studied yesterday.* |
| Past Progressive | indicates an action that was going on in the past | *She was studying in the library.* |
| Past Perfect | indicates an action further in the past than another action in the past | *She had studied hard before she wrote the exam.* |
| Past Perfect Progressive | indicates an action that was happening further in the past than another action in the past or an action in the past that was interrupted | *She had been studying hard before she wrote the exam.* |

## Future Tense

| Tense | Definition | Example |
|-------|------------|---------|
| Simple Future | indicates an action that will happen in the future | *She will study harder next time.* |
| Future Progressive | indicates an action that will be happening in the future | *She will be studying in the library tomorrow.* |
| Future Perfect | indicates an action that will be completed before another action | *She will have studied the whole book by the time she writes the exam* |
| Future Perfect Progressive | indicates an action that will be going on before another action | *She will have been studying for three weeks by the time she finishes.* |

| Examples | Erica *lifted* <u>the book</u>. [Erica lifted *what*? The book.] |
| | Richard *loves* <u>Flora</u>. [Richard loves *whom*? Flora.] |

If a verb does not require additional information to complete its meaning, it is intransitive. Be careful: additional information may be adverbial, which does not complete the meaning of the verb but simply modifies it.

| Examples | Erica *lifted*. [This statement is incomplete. You naturally ask, "Erica lifted *what*?" Therefore, the verb *lift* is transitive.] |
| | Janpreet *daydreamed* all morning. [*All morning* adds information but is not necessary to complete the statement. If you take it out—"Janpreet *daydreamed*"—the sentence still makes sense.] |

**Linking verbs** connect a subject with its **complement**.

| Examples | Trevor *is* Canadian. |

A **subject complement** is a noun that renames the subject or an adjective that describes the subject.

| Examples | I am *full*. [*Full* is an adjective describing the subject, *I*.] |
| | The book is *a bestseller* [*A bestseller* is a noun renaming the subject, *the book*.] |

Common linking verbs include *to be*, *seem*, *become*, *appear*, *look*, *grow*, and *remain*.

| Examples | That guy *appears* nice when you first meet him. |
| | The seed *grew to be* a massive tree. |
| | He *remains* single, but he *seems* happy. |

## Verb Voice

The **voice** of a verb indicates whether the subject of the sentence performs the action (**active voice**) or is acted upon (**passive voice**).

**Active voice.** The subject of the sentence performs the action.

| Example | The student wrote the exam. [The subject (*student*) performs the action (*wrote*).] |

**Passive voice.** The subject receives the action. Passive voice construction always requires a form of *be* plus the past participle.

| Example | The exam was written by the student. [The subject (*exam*) does not perform the action (*was written*).] |

Both the active and passive voices are grammatical; however, in many writing situations, the active voice is preferred (see "Choose the Right Voice" on page 68).

## Verbals

A **verbal** is a form of verb that is used as a noun, adjective, or adverb. It cannot stand alone as the main verb of a sentence because it serves as a noun or a modifier rather than as a verb.

There are three kinds of verbals: infinites, gerunds, and participles.

**Infinitives** function as nouns, adjectives, or adverbs.

Examples              I want *to leave*. [Noun.]
The student found the article difficult *to read*. [Adverb.]
The place *to practice* is the sports field. [Adjective.]

**Gerunds** function as nouns. Gerunds have the same form as the progressive tense (the infinitive form of the verb without *to*, plus *-ing*).

Examples              *Eating* is fun.
Her favourite activities are *reading* and *swimming*, but she thinks *dancing* is good fun, too.

**Participles** function as adjectives. Participles are of two types: **present participles** and **past participles.** Present participles have the same form as the progressive tense (the infinitive form of the verb without *to*, plus *-ing*). **Past participles** take a variety of forms, depending on the verb; most end in *-ed*; irregular past participles often end in *-en* (*broken, frozen, shaken*).

Examples              *Flying* badgers are rare. [Present participle.]
He listened to the *whistling* boy. [Present participle.]
She looked with pleasure at her freshly *weeded* garden [Past participle, regular.]
The *hidden* driveway caused problems. [Past participle, irregular.]

Note that present participles and gerunds are distinguished by their role in the sentence as either nouns or adjectives.

## Prepositions

**Prepositions** connect a noun or pronoun to another word in a sentence. Common prepositions include the following words or phrases: *in, on, under, with, without, in spite of, outside, inside, above, below, behind.*

A preposition is followed by a noun or pronoun (the object of the preposition). The preposition plus noun or pronoun forms a **prepositional phrase.** Prepositional phrases usually function as adjectives or adverbs. That is, they modify other elements in the sentence.

Example              Chris sat *in* the tree *on* the island *across* the river. [*In the tree* functions as an adverb modifying *sat*; *on the island* functions as an adjective modifying *the tree*; *across the river* functions as an adjective modifying *the island*]

The role of prepositions is simple, but their correct use can be complex. There is no way of predicting when a particular preposition will be used with a particular noun. For example, we talk of going *into* town, being *in* town, going *to* town, or hanging *around* town. Each preposition tells us something different about our relationship to the town.

The correct use of prepositions can be difficult to master. There are many websites and language-learning textbooks that can help you learn how to use prepositions and prepositional phrases correctly and idiomatically.

# Conjunctions

**Conjunctions** join words, phrases, and clauses. There are four kinds of conjunctions: coordinating conjunctions, correlative conjunctions, subordinating conjunctions, and conjunctive adverbs.

**Coordinating conjunctions** join grammatically equal words, phrases, and clauses to create compound constructions. There are seven coordinating conjunctions: *for*, *and*, *nor*, *but*, *or*, *yet*, and *so*. You can remember them by their initials: FANBOYS.

Example        It had become late *and* cold before Beth *and* Alannah arrived, *so* we got blankets *and* slept.

- The first coordinating conjunction joins two adjectives (*late* and *cold*).
- The second joins two subjects of the verb (*Beth* and *Alannah*).
- The third joins two independent clauses (*It had become late and cold before Beth and Alannah arrived* and *so we got blankets and slept*).
- The fourth joins the two verbs of the second clause (*got* and *slept*).

**Correlative conjunctions** work the same as coordinating conjunctions but use pairs of words or phrases, including *neither/nor, both/and, not only/but also, as/as,* and so forth.

Examples        We are *neither* tired *nor* cold.
                     The article was *not only* dull *but also* pointless.
                     He is *as* fit *as* a fiddle.

**Subordinating conjunctions** link a subordinate clause to an independent clause. Some examples of subordinating conjunctions are *because, before, since, while, although, if, until, when, after, as*, and *as if*.

Example        *After* Katie and Joanna arrived, the party became raucous.
                   **Subordinate clause:** *After* [subordinating conjunction] Katie and Joanna arrived,
                   **Independent clause:** the party became raucous.

**Conjunctive adverbs** join two independent clauses; they are preceded by a semicolon and followed by a comma. Make sure the conjunctive adverb joins two *independent* clauses before using a semicolon, or it will be grammatically incorrect. Common conjunctive adverbs include *therefore, moreover, thus, consequently*, and *however*.

Example        Andria did not arrive until eight o'clock; *consequently*, she missed Annalise's caramel desserts.

# Interjections

**Interjections** express strong feelings and are almost always set off by punctuation, usually a comma or exclamation point. They are not necessary for the grammatical structure of the sentence, unless they make up the entire sentence.

Examples        *Ha!* He fell for it, *eh?*
                   *Oh,* did you find your socks?

## Phrases

A **phrase** is a group of words that acts as a single part of speech, usually a noun, an adjective, or an adverb.

The three main types of phrases are prepositional phrases, participial phrases, and gerund phrases.

**Prepositional phrases** begin with a preposition followed by a noun or pronoun. They always function as either adjectives, giving more information about a noun in the sentence, or adverbs, giving more information about an adjective, a verb, or another adverb.

Prepositional phrase  He left the room <u>without speaking</u> [*Without speaking* acts as an adverb modifying *left*.]

**Participial phrases** always act as adjectives. They are formed with either the present participle (the *-ing* form) or the past participle of a verb.

Participial phrase  <u>Looking back</u>, he wondered what had happened.
He read the book <u>taken from the library</u>.

**Gerund phrases** always act as nouns. They use the present participle of a verb, but they function as a noun and can be used in any place in a sentence where a noun could be used.

Gerund phrase  *Learning grammar* can be tedious.
She remembered *asking him about the exam*.

## SENTENCES

The **sentence** is the basic unit of expression in English. It expresses a grammatically complete thought, which requires two parts: a subject and a predicate.

The **subject** names the thing that the sentence is about.

The **predicate** says something about the subject.

Examples  Mary laughed. [*Mary* is the subject; *laughed* is the predicate.]
Jo kicked the ball. [*Jo* is the subject; *kicked the ball* is the predicate.]
The article that he read for class was much longer than he expected. [*The article that he read for class* is the subject; *was much longer than he expected is the predicate.]*

## Clauses

A **clause** is a group of words that contains both a subject and a predicate. The two main types of clauses are **independent** and **subordinate** (**dependent**).

**Independent clauses** are complete sentences; they can stand on their own.

Example  *Learning grammar is difficult,* which is why many people don't do it.

[*Learning grammar is difficult* can stand alone without what follows.]

**Subordinate** or **dependent clauses** must be linked to an independent clause that completes the idea.

Example                Learning grammar is difficult, *which is why many people don't do it.*
                       [*which is why many people don't do it* contains both a subject and a predicate, but it doesn't make sense on its own.]

## Types of Sentences

There are four types of sentences: **simple**, **compound**, **complex**, and **compound-complex**.

**Simple sentences** are made up of a single independent clause. They do not have any subordinate clauses, but they can include phrases.

Examples               *We* went shopping.
                       [*subject* and predicate]
                       *We* went shopping **at Bingo's Food Mart**.
                       [*subject*, predicate, and **adverbial phrase**]

**Compound sentences** are made up of two or more independent clauses, joined by punctuation or both punctuation and a coordinating conjunction. They do not include any subordinate clauses, but they can include phrases.

Examples               *We* went shopping; *we* bought nothing.
                       [*subject* predicate **semicolon** *subject* predicate]
                       *We* went shopping; **however,** *we* bought nothing.
                       [*subject* predicate **semicolon** **conjunctive adverb** comma *subject* predicate]
                       *We* went shopping, **and** *we* bought nothing.
                       [*subject* predicate **comma** **coordinating conjunction** *subject* predicate]

**Complex sentences** are made up of one independent clause and one or more subordinate clauses. They can include phrases.

Examples               *Whoever went shopping* bought nothing.
                       [*subject,* a subordinate clause predicate]
                       *Although we went shopping,* we bought nothing.
                       [*subordinate clause* **comma** independent clause]
                       *Although we went shopping,* we bought nothing because there wasn't anything good.
                       [*subordinate clause* **comma** independent clause subordinate clause]

**Compound-complex sentences** are made up of two or more independent clauses and one or more subordinate clauses. They can include phrases.

Examples               *Although we went shopping,* we bought nothing at the shop, so we bought lunch instead.
                       [*subordinate clause* **comma** independent clause adjectival

prepositional phrase **comma** <u>independent clause</u>]
*Although we went shopping,* <u>we bought nothing</u>: nothing was worth buying.
[*subordinate clause* **comma** <u>independent clause</u> **colon** independent clause]

# COMMON ERRORS IN GRAMMAR

In this section, you can learn how to fix some of the most common errors students make in their writing. If you are struggling with any of the terminology in this section, refer to the previous section on parts of speech and sentence construction for an explanation.

If you need more help with any of these errors, visit a Writing Centre tutor or use online exercises to practise.

## Subject-Verb Agreement

Verbs must agree with their subjects in number (singular or plural).

| | |
|---|---|
| Incorrect | The book on the shelf belong to me. [*Book* is singular, but *belong* is the plural form of the verb.] |
| Correct | The book on the shelf belongs to me. [The singular form of the verb agrees with the singular subject.] |

**Compound subjects** are subjects that contain more than one noun or pronoun joined by *and*. They require the plural form of the verb.

| | |
|---|---|
| Compound subject | Biology and mathematics are my favourite subjects. |

Some subjects that appear to be compounds are treated as singular. For example, in the sentence *His friend and constant companion is his dog,* the two nouns in the subject (*His friend and constant companion*) refer to the same thing and are treated as a singular subject.

## Noun-Pronoun Agreement

Pronouns must agree with the nouns they refer to (their **antecedents**) in number (singular or plural) and person (first, second, or third).

| | |
|---|---|
| Incorrect | What should *a student* do if *they* are late with an assignment? [*A student* is third-person singular, but *they* is third-person plural.] |
| Correct | What should students do if they are late with an assignment? |
| Incorrect | *He* needs to know what *you're* supposed to do. [*He* is third-person singular, but *you* is second person.] |
| Correct | He needs to know what he is supposed to do |

For more advice on avoiding noun-pronoun agreement errors, see "Use the Correct Person" on page 73.

## Article Use

The use of articles in English can be hard to explain by rules. Whether a noun takes the definite article, the indefinite article, or no article often depends on the context and the type of noun.

### General Guidelines for Using Articles

**Use *a/an***

- before countable nouns: *an ant, a dream, an art show, a detail, a university, an umbrella*)

- if you generalize about a whole group or class of things: *A computer makes a student's life easier, but a dog is a faithful companion.*

- if you mean *a kind of*: *Jenny wants to try a cheese she hasn't tried before. John tried a popcorn I never imagined existed: grass-flavoured.*

- the first time that you mention something—after that, the noun becomes definite, so use *the*: *I saw a movie last night. A tall guy sat in front of me. The movie was scary, and the guy crouched down in his seat.*

- before class nouns modified by adjectives: *Kimiko had an odd experience in the library.*

**Do not use a/an**

- if an object is common in a cultural situation even though it hasn't been mentioned before: *The mail wasn't there when I picked up the newspaper.*

- before plural nouns: *apples, schools*

- before uncountable nouns: *information*

- before unique nouns: *sun*

- before superlatives: *biggest, worst, fastest*

**Use *the***

- before unique nouns: *the sun*; superlatives: *the best book;* nouns modified by prepositional phrases: *the University of Utopia, the ninth of September* (but *September 9*); nouns modified by participles: *the polishing process, the polished cabinet;* and nouns made particular in context: *She is the member of Parliament to whom I wrote the letter.*

- if you want a single noun to mean a whole species or group: *The cat is an aloof animal.*

- before public institutions: *the Library of Congress, the Royal British Columbia Museum;* theatres: *the Royal, the Roxy;* hotels: *the Ritz, the Dominion;* or newspapers: *The New York Times, The Globe and Mail*

- before inventions: *Who invented the computer mouse?*

- before key historical events: *the Ming Dynasty, the Cultural Revolution, the Second World War, the Industrial Revolution*

- before some geographical names: *the Antarctic;* plural place names, such as those referring to islands, states, or provinces: *the USA, the British Isles, the Philippines, the Hawaiian Islands, the Bahamas, the Falklands, the Netherlands;* parts of cities:

the East End, the Downtown East Side; rivers: the St. Lawrence, the Fraser, the Yangtze; seas: the Pacific Ocean, the Mediterranean, the Red Sea; mountain chains: the Rockies, the Himalayas; canals: the Suez, the Panama; deserts (the Sahara, the Kalahari; winds: the Mistral, the Chinook

- before proper nouns used as modifiers: the Chinese New Year decorations, the Valentine's Day dance, the Robbie Burns' Night dinner

**Do not use *the***

- before proper nouns if they are not definite: Hanukkah; before abstract nouns if you are talking about them generally: beauty (but, The beauty of this movie is the camerawork); or before nouns behaving as abstract nouns: before kindergarten

- before plural non-specific nouns: computers are useless because ...; midterms create ...

- before geographical names of continents (Europe), countries (Japan), cities (Seoul), lakes (Elk Lake, Lake Huron), individual mountains (Mount Robson, Mount Everest), or streets, avenues, and so forth (Yates, Main, Shelbourne)

## Shifts in Verb Tense

Correct verb tense is essential to meaning. It helps the reader understand when things happen in relation to the time of writing and in relation to other events. Consider the difference in meaning between these two sentences:

| Original | He leaves before she finishes her presentation and goes directly to the airport, but the plane departs. |
|---|---|
| Revised | He left before she had finished her presentation and went directly to the airport, but the plane had departed. |

In the first sentence, everything seems to be happening at the same time; in the second, the correct verb tense allows us to understand the sequence of events.

A common error with verb tense is shifting the tense within the same sentence or paragraph. Shifts that are unnecessary or incorrect are confusing to the reader.

| Original | If Armand had known she is coming, he can take some time off. They could visit the museum. |
|---|---|
| Revised | If Armand had known she was coming, he could have taken time off to show her around the university. They could have visited the museum. |

In the first sentence, it is unclear which verb tense is incorrect, but the result is confusing to the reader.

## Irregular Verbs

Most verbs in English follow a standard pattern. New verbs like text follow that pattern: both the past tense and past participle end in -ed (texted). But some older verbs have irregular past tense or past participle forms. These forms cannot be guessed at because they do not follow the usual pattern.

The most common irregular verbs are also some of the most commonly used verbs in English.

There are many more irregular English verbs than in the table below; complete lists can be found online or in language guides. The only way to learn them is to memorize them.

## Irregular Verbs

| Base | Past | Past participle |
|------|------|-----------------|
| be | was, were | been |
| become | became | become |
| begin | began | begun |
| bring | brought | brought |
| choose | chose | chosen |
| come | came | come |
| do | did | done |
| drink | drank | drunk |
| find | found | found |
| go | went | gone |
| have | had | had |
| keep | kept | kept |
| know | knew | known |
| make | made | made |
| say | said | said |
| speak | spoke | spoken |
| take | took | taken |
| teach | taught | taught |
| write | wrote | written |

## Dangling Modifiers

Dangling modifiers are words or phrases that modify nouns or pronouns that are not clearly stated. They frequently occur at the beginning of a sentence.

Dangling

<u>Walking barefoot through the meadow</u>, the grass tickled my feet.
<u>While waiting for the bus one morning</u>, a bird sat next to me on the bench.

According to these sentences, the grass was walking barefoot and a bird was waiting for the bus. Notice that the subjects of *walking* and *waiting* have been omitted. To correct a dangling modifier, make sure that the noun or pronoun they modify is the subject of the independent clause that follows, or add the subject to the phrase, turning it into a subordinate clause.

| Correct | Walking barefoot through the meadow, *I* felt the grass tickle my feet. |
| | While *I* was waiting for the bus one morning, a bird sat next to me on the bench. |

## Misplaced Modifiers

Misplaced modifiers are words or phrases that are placed too far from the words they modify.

| Confusing | Lying on his desk, James noticed the work he had left to do. |
| | The instructor understood the point the student was trying to make quickly. |

Unless James was lying on his desk and the student was making a point quickly, the modifiers *lying on his desk* and *quickly* have to be moved.

| Revised | James noticed the work he had left to do, which was lying on his desk. |
| | The instructor quickly understood the point the student was trying to make. |

## Sentence Fragments

A **sentence fragment** is a sentence that is missing either a subject, a predicate, or both. A dependent clause on its own is also a sentence fragment because it does not express a complete thought.

| Fragments | Then goes to work in the evenings. |
| | If you are alone and you need help. |

The first example is missing a subject, the person who goes to work in the evenings. The second example is a dependent clause, which must be attached to an independent clause. To fix these problems, you need to complete each fragment so that the sentence can stand on its own:

| Revised | Then, Francine goes to work in the evenings. |
| | If you are alone and you need help, a cell phone could save your life. |

## Comma Splices

A **comma splice** occurs when you join two complete sentences together with a comma.

| Comma Splice | Oil spills harm sensitive ecosystems, they also damage coastal wetlands. |

You can fix a comma splice in a number of ways: use a semicolon (;) instead of a comma; use a period instead of a comma; use a coordinating conjunction like *and* between the two sentences; or rewrite the sentence.

| Revised | Oil spills harm sensitive ecosystems. They also damage coastal wetlands. |

Oil spills harm sensitive ecosystems and damage coastal wetlands.

## Run-on Sentences

A **run-on sentence** contains multiple subjects and predicates but not the necessary punctuation or joining words.

Run-on Sentence    Twenty-four crew members are aboard the International Space Station the crew performed tests on a new telerobotic system they expect the system will have applications on Earth.

Run-on sentences should be broken up into smaller sentences or joined using the appropriate punctuation or conjunctions.

Revised    Twenty-four crew members are aboard the International Space Station. The crew performed tests on a new telerobotic system that they expect will have applications on Earth.

# Punctuation, Spelling, and Mechanics

## PUNCTUATION

The rules of English punctuation can—and do—fill books. But the basic rules, which cover most of the writing you will do as a student, can be summed up in a few pages, as they are here. Learning how to punctuate will help you write more clearly and correctly, and it will give you practice in paying close attention to your words.

### End punctuation ( . / ! / ? )

Three punctuation marks indicate the end of a sentence: the **period**, **question mark**, and **exclamation mark.**

Use a period at the end of a normal sentence, including an indirect question.

> Browne argues that Hitler was a socialist.

> Huang asked Browne what he meant by his assertion.

Use a question mark after a direct question.

> Was Browne really asserting this, or was he simply attempting to get a reaction?

Use an exclamation mark after an emphatic statement, interjection, or command.

> Scholars should not make remarks they don't truly believe!

### Comma ( , )

Use a comma to separate independent clauses linked by a coordinating conjunction (*and, but, or, nor, so, for, yet*).

> Herpes simplex 1 is transmitted orally, <u>and</u> herpes simplex 2 is transmitted sexually.

> Anthropologists describe cultures, <u>but</u> these descriptions sometimes represent anthropology's own cultural bias.

Use a comma to set off most introductory words, phrases, or clauses.

> <u>Although men were traditionally more likely to go to university,</u> women are now the majority of university students.

> <u>Uncertain about the side-effects of the medication,</u> he declined treatment.

> <u>Near the plains of the Tigris-Euphrates,</u> farming began to transform social relations.

> <u>Actually,</u> the engine will be modified as little as possible.

Use a comma to set off non-restrictive phrases or clauses.

> His argument<u>, which he still defends vigorously,</u> has been refuted by his colleagues.

> The tournament was held in summer<u>, when many people were away</u>.

Use a comma to set off phrases expressing contrast.

> Methane, <u>not oxygen,</u> sustains the anaerobic microorganisms found on the sea floor.

Use a comma between items in a series or list. (Note that not all editorial styles follow this rule.)

> Byron uses <u>punctuation, aberrations in rhyme scheme, and variations in meter</u> to emphasize the shock of losing the nightingale.

> The invasion was based on <u>economics, politics, and ethics</u>.

Use a comma between coordinate adjectives.

> Henry VIII led a <u>philandering, overindulgent</u> life.

> She bought a <u>lighter, faster</u> bicycle.

Use a comma in dates, addresses, place names, and numbers of more than four digits (unless the editorial style you are using does not follow this rule).

> The Battle of Passchendaele did not end until <u>November 6, 1917</u>.

> The book was published by Baldwin and Cradock, <u>47 Paternoster Row, London</u>.

> Beatrix Potter paid <u>£2,805</u> for Hill Top with the royalties from her books.

Use a comma with identifying words before or after a quotation.

> Byron <u>wrote,</u> "I will have nothing to do with your immortality."

> "To jaw-jaw is better than to war-war,<u>" quipped Winston Churchill.</u>

Do not use commas when a quotation ends in an exclamation mark or question mark.

> "If men are to live, why die at all<u>?" he continued.</u>

Do not use a comma when a quotation or the clause containing the quotation is introduced by "that."

> The report stipulates <u>that "the issues could not be addressed by changes"</u> to Bill C-38.

## Semicolon ( ; )

Use a semicolon between related main clauses not joined by a coordinating conjunction.

> Methane's chemical formula is CH4; it is therefore an alkane.

Use a semicolon between independent clauses joined by *however, thus, therefore*, or other conjunctive adverb.

> Carbon monoxide is colourless, odorless, and poisonous; therefore, it can be extremely dangerous.

When the adverb falls somewhere other than at the beginning of the clause, set it off with a comma.

> Infected ants are carried from the colony; the spores, however, often waft back to infect the rest.

Use a semicolon to separate items in a series if they are long or contain commas.

Byron travelled to Sestos, Greece; Geneva, Switzerland; and Venice, Italy.

## Apostrophe ( ' )

Use the apostrophe to indicate the possessive case for nouns and indefinite pronouns.

Add –'s to form the possessive case of singular nouns (including those ending in –s), indefinite pronouns, and the possessive case of plural nouns not ending in –s.

The *book's* cover was yellow, but it was not the *Yellow Book*.

*Wilde's* trial did not end happily for the flamboyant author.

Homosexual *men's* acts were punishable by law until 1967.

The *children's* stories of Oscar Wilde remain popular today.

John *Ellis's* contributions to phenomenology are numerous.

*Phosphorus's* atomic weight is 30.97 atomic mass units.

Add only an apostrophe to form the possessive case of *plural* nouns ending in –s.

The *physicists'* worries grew when the atomic bomb was detonated.

In several *weeks'* time, two bombs would be dropped on Japan.

When two or more words show individual possession, add –'s to each of them. If they show joint possession, add –'s to the last word only.

| Individual possession | Anne's and Charlotte's novels [meaning each sister's novels] were very different. |
|---|---|
| Joint possession | Hilder and Singh's article [meaning the article co-authored by Hilder and Singh] has been widely accepted. |

Apostrophes are NOT used to form plurals, present tense verbs, or possessives of personal pronouns.

| Incorrect | The book's belong to her. / He believe's her story. /The books are their's. |
|---|---|
| Correct | The books belong to her. / He believes her story. / The books are theirs. |

Use an apostrophe to indicate omission in a standard contraction.

| Words | Contraction |
|---|---|
| it is | it's |
| he is | he's |
| they are | they're |
| you are | you're |
| who is | who's |
| does not | doesn't |
| were not | weren't |

| | |
|---|---|
| class of 1998 | class of '98 |
| of the clock | o'clock |

Do not confuse contractions with possessive personal pronouns.

Incorrect You're admiration for Wilde's work is based entirely upon it's wit.

Correct Your admiration for Wilde's work is based entirely upon its wit.

| **Contraction** | **Possessive Pronoun** |
|---|---|
| it's | its |
| they're | their |
| you're | your |
| who's | whose |

Use an apostrophe plus –*s* to form the plurals of letters, numerals, and words named as words.

There were no if's, and's, or but's about it: Wilde simply stated, "Either that wallpaper goes, or I do" before he died.

To be "at 6's and 7's" is a colloquial British phrase; it means that one is confused. (Note: written "sixes and sevens" with no apostrophes if words are used.)

There are four s's in Mississippi.

Exception: The apostrophe is omitted when referring to years.

Incorrect He was born in the late 1980's.

Correct He was born in the late 1980s.

Do not use an apostrophe when you pluralize an abbreviation that does not take internal periods: DVDs, PhDs, MDs.

## Quotation Marks ( " " )

The following rules apply to the general use of quotation marks. For details on how to use quotations within your academic writing, see "Quoting" on page 41.

Use double quotation marks to mark direct quotations.

Einstein called pure mathematics "the poetry of ideas."

Do not use quotation marks with indirect quotations.

Einstein believed that mathematics was similar to poetry.

Use single quotation marks around a quotation within a quotation.

Dr. Mazumder wrote, "To use Malcolm Gladwell's phrase, we have reached 'the tipping point.'"

Put quotation marks around the titles of works that are parts of other works. These include the titles of songs, short stories, short poems, articles in a periodical, essays, episodes of a TV or radio program, and chapters or subdivisions of a book.

Lewis's "The Case for Christianity" was first aired in 1943 and was later published as part of *Mere Christianity*.

Use quotation marks to enclose words being defined or used in a special sense.

"Quarks" are fundamental elementary particles that have six "flavours": up, down, charm, strange, top (sometimes "truth"), and bottom (sometimes "beauty").

Place periods and commas inside the closing quotation mark.

She referred to his employment as "temporary."

He quoted from "The Waste Land," not realizing I had never read it.

Place colons and semicolons outside quotation marks.

Louis XIV was known as "the Sun King"; his reign is often looked upon as a golden age.

Place dashes, question marks, and exclamation points inside quotation marks only if they belong to the quotation.

Keats asks, "What men or gods are these?"

When a dash, question mark, or exclamation point applies only to the larger sentence, not to the quotation, place it outside quotation marks—again, with no other punctuation.

Is Puck's line "if we spirits have offended" or "if we shadows have offended"?

## Colon ( : )

Use the colon following an independent clause to introduce further information. A colon often introduces a list, but it can also introduce a single word, a phrase, a sentence, or more.

Use a colon to introduce a concluding explanation, series, appositive, or long or formal quotation.

The atomic number indicates the number of only one particle: protons.

The opening of Psalm 32 often strikes readers as contradicting other parts of the Bible: "Blessed is he whose transgressions are forgiven, whose sins are covered."

Use a colon to separate titles and subtitles, the subdivisions of time, and the parts of biblical citations.

Moore's essay "Byron: Hedonist and Aesthete" received international praise.

Wilde died in Paris at 10:00 a.m. on 30 November 1900.

"He that endureth to the end shall be saved" (Matthew 10:22).

Do not use the colon unless it follows an independent clause.

| | |
|---|---|
| Incorrect | The only book she liked was: *The Life of Pi*. |
| Correct | The only book she liked was *The Life of Pi*. |
| | Xinyi liked only one book: *The Life of Pi*. |
| Incorrect | There are many political ideologies, including: liberalism, conservatism, and socialism. |

| Correct | There are many political ideologies, including liberalism, conservatism, and socialism. |
|---|---|
| | There are many political ideologies: the most widely practiced are liberalism, conservatism, and socialism. |

## Dash ( — )

The dash is used to set off words, phrases, and clauses that interrupt the rest of the sentence in which they appear.

Use a dash or dashes to emphasize non-restrictive elements.

> Wilde's favourite male companion—Lord Alfred Douglas—used Wilde most abominably.

> He was jailed in spite of—or perhaps because of—his fame.

Use a dash to set off series and explanations.

> Wilde is most famous for three things—his wit, his fashion, and his sexual orientation.

Don't use dashes where commas, semicolons, or periods are more appropriate. Overuse of the dash is distracting and minimizes emphasis.

## Parentheses ( )

Use parentheses to enclose non-essential elements within sentences.

Use parentheses to enclose parenthetical expressions—including explanations, facts, digressions, and examples—that may be helpful or interesting but are not essential to meaning.

> Einstein is most famous for his theory that mass can be converted to energy ($E=mc^2$).

Note: Don't put a comma before a parenthetical expression enclosed in parentheses.

| Incorrect | Einstein's theory, ($E=mc^2$) is known all over the world. |
|---|---|
| Correct | Einstein's theory ($E=mc^2$) is known all over the world. |

Place a comma or period falling after a parenthetical expression outside the closing parenthesis.

> Einstein is best known for one equation ($E=mc^2$), which is recognized everywhere.

When it falls between other sentences, a complete sentence enclosed in parentheses is capitalized and punctuated as a sentence within the parentheses.

> Space-time suggests that time is fused to space. (This creates a continuum.)

Use parentheses to enclose letters and figures labelling items in lists within sentences.

> The obsolete adjective *spackly* had three meanings: (1) forcefully, (2) swiftly, and (3) intelligently.

# SPELLING

English spelling is not easy to master. Because English spelling bears little relationship to English pronunciation (consider the difference between the pronunciation and the spelling of words like *laugh, thorough, height*, and *foreign*), spelling has to be learned rather than guessed at. As an academic writer, you are expected to spell correctly and may lose marks for spelling errors in your writing, so becoming a better speller is well worth the effort.

## Spelling Tips

**Look it up.** The best way to make sure you have spelled a word correctly is to look it up. If you cannot find the word, try spelling it another way. Online dictionaries will suggest spellings if you have entered a word incorrectly. Once you have looked up a word, ensure that the meaning is correct: English contains many homonyms (words that sound the same but are spelled differently) that have different meanings.

**Make lists.** When you come across a word you don't know, write it and its meaning down. Look over these words periodically to help remember how they are spelled.

**Write out words.** Writing a difficult word over and over can help you memorize its spelling.

**Make up sentences and memory aids.** You can help your memory by using your own learning aids, or mnemonics. For example, the sentence "Bu*sin*ess is no *sin*" may help you remember the spelling of *business*.

**Learn spelling tricks.** Tricks like "*i* before *e* except after *c* and in words that say *eh*, as in *neighbour* or *weigh*" are useful, but remember that there are exceptions (like *protein*). Some words simply need to be memorized. Know tricks like the above rhyme, but don't rely on them too much.

**Take words apart.** A word like *indispensable* includes the word *dispense*. Breaking up the entire word into smaller words makes the word less intimidating—you will probably find that you know the spelling of many root words.

**Sound the word out.** This doesn't always work (consider the word *Wednesday*), but it can help with long words like *heterodoxy*, or even *antidisestablishmentarianism*.

**Pay attention to pronunciation.** If you say a word incorrectly, you will likely also spell it incorrectly. The word *pronunciation*, for example, is often incorrectly spoken and written *pro**noun**ciation*. Use the pronunciation guides provided by online dictionaries.

**Be familiar with homonyms.** Homonyms—words that sound the same but have different meanings—are often a source of spelling mistakes. Learn common homonym groups like *to/too/two, whose/who's*, and *they're/their/there*.

**Differentiate between word forms.** Know, for example, the difference between the verb *advise* and the noun *advice*. (Some words keep the same spelling in different forms, like the verb *control* and noun *control*.)

**Learn spelling rules.** Some common spelling rules are listed below.

## Some Commonly Misspelled Words

| | | | |
|---|---|---|---|
| absence | desperate | knowledge | psychology |
| accidentally | dilemma | laboratory | pursue |
| accommodate | disappear | liaison | questionnaire |
| achievement | disastrous | license | queue |
| acknowledge | discipline | lieutenant | realize |
| acquire | dissatisfied | medieval | receipt |
| adolescence | doesn't | millionaire | receive |
| aggressive | ecstasy | miniscule | recommend |
| amateur | eighth | mischievous | reference |
| analysis | embarrass | monastery | referring |
| analyze | environment | mysticism | relevance |
| anxious | erroneous | necessary | religious |
| apparent | exaggerate | ninety | repetition |
| appearance | excellent | ninth | resistance |
| approximately | exhilaration | noticeable | rhythm |
| attendant | exist | nuclear | ridiculous |
| auxiliary | existence | nucleus | sacrilegious |
| believe | fallacy | occasion(ally) | schedule |
| business | familiar | occur | schism |
| calendar | fascinating | occurred | secretary |
| caricature | February | occurrence | seize |
| cemetery | feudal | omission | sensible |
| changeable | fictitious | omitted | separate |
| character | forcibly | opinion | sergeant |
| column | foreign | opportunity | shepherd |
| committee | forfeit | outrageous | shining |
| comparatively | forty | parallel | siege |
| conceivable | gauge | perceive | similar |
| condemn | government | perform | souvenir |
| congratulations | governor | permanent | strength |
| conscience | grammar | permissible | success |
| conscientious | guarantee | perseverance | supersede |
| conscious | guidance | persuasive | suppress |
| consensus | height | peruse | synonym |
| consistent | humorous | pilgrimage | temperament |
| constant | humour | playwright | thorough |
| continuous | hypocrisy | possession | tragedy |
| copyright | immediately | preceding | twelfth |
| counsellor | incidentally | prejudice | tyranny |
| courteous | independent | prevalent | unnecessary |
| criticism | indispensable | privilege | vacuum |
| curiosity | intelligence | proceed | vengeance |
| curriculum | irrelevant | professor | villain |
| deceive | irresistible | pronounce | Wednesday |
| definite | jeopardy | pronunciation | weird |
| desirable | kindergarten | psychiatry | written |

## Spelling Rules

### Adding an Ending After a Final e
- Drop the final *e* in a word when adding an ending that begins with a vowel (*bike/biking* or *fame/famous*).
- Keep the final (silent) *e* when adding an ending that begins with a consonant (*love/loveless*).
- Keep the *e* if it follows a soft *c* or *g* (*courage/courageous*; *notice/noticeable*).
- Keep the final *e* to avoid confusion (*dying a death* vs. *dyeing a shirt*).

### Adding an Ending After a Final y
- Change the final *y* to an *i* when it follows a consonant (*worry/worried; happy/happiness*).
- Keep the final *y* if it follows a vowel or if the ending is *–ing* (*day/days; cry/crying*).

### Doubling Consonants
Double the final consonant before an ending that begins with a vowel, such as *–ing*, if
- it follows a single short vowel (*pop/popping*), or
- the syllable directly before the ending is stressed (*admit/admitted*).

Otherwise, the ending is added without any change (*edit/editing; credit/credited*).

### Attaching Prefixes
When attaching prefixes such as *dis–, un–, ir–,* or *mis–*, do not drop a letter from the original word.

> *dis + satisfied = dissatisfied*
>
> *un + necessary = unnecessary*
>
> *ir + replaceable = irreplaceable*
>
> *mis + spell = misspell*

### Forming Plurals
- Add *-s* to most words to form the plural (*cat/cats*).
- For words ending in *-ch, -sh, -s, -z,* and *-x,* form the plural by adding *-es* (*kisses, lunches, foxes*).
- For words ending in *y,* add *-ies* if the *y* follows a consonant (*party/parties*).
- For most words ending in *-f* or *-fe,* form the plural by adding *-ves* (*calf/calves; life/lives*).
- For Latin-derived words such as *alumnus,* form the plural by adding *-i* (*alumni*) or *-a* (*data*). Note that *media* and *phenomena* are already plural; use the singular when appropriate: *One <u>phenomenon</u> of the last half of the twentieth century was the dominance of television as a <u>medium</u>.*
- Add plural endings to the end of the word for solid compound words (*spoonfuls*). Add plural endings to the noun if the word is a hyphenated compound (*mothers-in-law*).

- *Data* is the plural of *datum*. Grammatically speaking, data should take a plural verb: *The data are inconclusive* rather than *The data is inconclusive*. However, in recent usage, *data* often takes a singular verb. If you are in doubt, choose the plural verb.

- Some plurals are unpredictable and have to be memorized (*child/children*).

## Variant Spellings

Some English words have more than one spelling. Most differences are between American and British spelling. Canadian spelling has been influenced by both. Below are some examples of common variants. (For preferred Canadian spellings, refer to a Canadian dictionary.)

| American | British | Canadian |
| --- | --- | --- |
| color | colour | colour |
| center | centre | centre |
| analyze | analyse | analyze |
| woolen | woollen | woollen |
| judgment | judgement | judgment |
| canceled | cancelled | cancelled |

## Using Hyphens

The **hyphen** is mainly used to form compound words—compound nouns and compound adjectives.

**Compound nouns** are nouns that consist of two or more words (*self-hatred, high school, dishwasher*). Some compound nouns require a hyphen, some are written as two words, and some are written as a single word. The only way to know for sure if a compound noun should be hyphenated is to look it up in a dictionary.

**Compound adjectives** are adjectives that consist of two or more words that together act as a single adjective. All words within a compound adjective are joined by hyphens (*a well-known author, just-in-time manufacturing, seven-part series*).

- When a compound adjective follows the noun, it does not require a hyphen (*the author is well known*).

- Use a hyphen in two-digit spelled-out numbers (*forty-five thousand, sixteen twenty-two, twenty-five*).

- Use a hyphen in numerical compound adjectives (*two-word adjective, 367-page document, eighteenth-century belief, ten-kilometre hike*). Note that when *century* is the noun rather than part of a compound adjective, there is no hyphen between it and the number preceding it (*mid-eighteenth-century belief* but *he married in the mid-eighteenth century*).

- Do not hyphenate numerical adjectives if the unit of measurement is abbreviated (*200 m sprint*).

- Do not hyphenate compound adjectives made of common open compound nouns (*high school grades, real estate boom*).

- Do not hyphenate a compound adjective if the first word is an adverb ending in *–ly* (*beautifully written book, richly detailed diagram*).

# MECHANICS

The term **mechanics** when used in the context of writing refers to the rules of written language that are concerned with how words appear on the page. Mechanics covers the use of abbreviations, numbers, capitals, and italics.

This section provides general advice about how to use mechanics properly within your writing; however, you should always consult a style guide (for example, MLA, APA) if your instructor has asked you to write in a particular style.

## Abbreviations

An **abbreviation** is a shortened form of a word or phrase (such as *Dr., PhD, USA, e.g.*). There are two types of abbreviations: acronyms and initialisms.

An **acronym** is an abbreviation made from the initial letters of words that is itself a word (for example, *SARS,* from severe acute respiratory syndrome; *AIDS,* from acquired immune deficiency syndrome).

An **initialism** is an abbreviation made from the initial letters of words that does not form a word (for example, *CBC,* from Canadian Broadcasting Corporation).

It is often best to give the abbreviated term—especially lesser known abbreviations—in full the first time you use it, placing the abbreviation in parentheses to ensure that your readers are familiar with the term. Well known abbreviations (such as *PhD* or *US*) can be used without first giving the term.

> The World Health Organization (WHO) sent out a directive to several countries that urged them to isolate all patients with Severe Acute Respiratory Syndrome (SARS) and to contact any member of the public who may have been in contact with those infected with the virus. WHO hopes that this will prevent the spread of the virus. The current number of deaths caused by SARS now stands at twenty-two, including four US citizens.

Generally, single-word abbreviations require periods at the end, and only letters that are capitalized in the original term are capitalized (*Dr.* for *Doctor, etc.* for *et cetera, Sept.* for *September, vols.* for *volumes*).

Initialisms and acronyms do not require periods and are usually capitalized (*UN* for *United Nations, HST* for *harmonized sales tax, AIDS* for *acquired immune deficiency syndrome*).

Latin abbreviations (for example, *i.e., etc., et al., e.g.*) should generally be reserved for use within parentheses or within citations. If you need to use them elsewhere, write out the equivalent phrase (for example, instead of *i.e.,* write *that is*).

Use business abbreviations (such as *corp., inc., ltd., bros.*) only if they appear in or are the official name of a company about which you are writing (*Warner Bros., AT&T*).

Periods can either be used within technical terms (*m.p.h.*) or left out (*mph*), but they should not appear after or within technical terms if they are not used between all letters of the technical term (not *mph.* or *mp.h*). Abbreviations of metric measurements do not take periods (for example, *km, cm, kg*).

## Numbers

When your writing includes numbers, you have a choice of using words or numerals. While some rules governing your choice are straightforward—years, for example, are always written as numerals—most others will depend on whether you are writing technical or non-technical text. They will also depend on whether you are following a particular academic style, like APA or MLA. If that is the case, your style guide will tell you in which contexts to use either words or numerals.

The following guidelines cover the most common rules for both technical and non-technical writing. If you are in doubt, find out which style your instructor wants you to use or, if you already know, check the style guide.

### General Rules

- Do not start a sentence with a numeral. Either write out the number or rearrange the sentence.

  Incorrect  118 scholarships were awarded to the top graduating students.

  Correct  One hundred and eighteen scholarships were awarded to the top graduating students.
  Of the graduating students, 118 received scholarships.

- Use numerals for percentages, dates, decimals, page numbers, scores, addresses, statistics, the time, exact monetary amounts, chapter numbers, and years (*chapter 7, page 43, 12 percent, scene 1, Deuteronomy 1:7, $2,378, 8 to 1, 76 Homeny Drive, 15 September 1953*).

- For numbers over a million, use a combination of numerals and words (*the global population is now 6.7 billion*).

### Numbers in Non-Technical Text

- In non-technical documents, spell out one- or two-word numbers (*twelve, ninety-nine*).

- Spell out units of measurement (*millilitres* not *mL*) except those expressed in longer phrases (*mph* may be used instead of *miles per hour*).

- For fractions, spell out or use numerals following the same rules as for whole numbers (*one-half, two-fifths, forty-three hundredths, 42/987*). As each style differs in the hyphenation of fractions, refer to your style guide as needed.

- Spell out amounts of money if the amount can be expressed in one or two words (*forty-five cents*).

- Write out number ranges (*ten to fifteen minutes,* not *10–15 minutes*).

  Examples  There were almost *two hundred* children at the hospital when it collapsed.

Over *twenty million* Canadians watched at least part of the
Olympics.
On *page 45*, the protagonist turned *fifty-three*.
The book cost *fifteen shillings*.
The house cost *$459,000*.

### Numbers in Technical (Scientific) Text

In technical documents, most numbers are written in numerals (*12*, not *twelve*). Numbers less than ten are written as words unless they are measurements.

- Avoid placing two unrelated numerals next to each other (instead of *12 1 cm blocks*, write *twelve 1 cm blocks*)

- If you are writing a decimal less than one, place a zero before the decimal point (*0.23*, not *.23*).

Examples           Muons are about *200* times heavier than electrons.
Your chances of getting AIDS are *1 in 125,562*.
The article was reviewed by *three* scientists.

## Capitals

The use of capitals can be confusing. Words of the kind that you are most used to seeing with capitals, like the names of people and countries, are easily identified as needing capitals. But other words, especially ones that are capitalized sometimes but not always, are more puzzling. Consider the difference between "the University of Victoria" and "the university that his mother attended." In the first case, "University" is part of a proper noun, which means it must be capitalized. In the second, "university" is a common noun, so it does not need a capital.

A second difficulty with capitals is that styles in capitalization have changed in recent times. We have gone from using capitals very freely to limiting their use. Many uses of capitals have fallen out of editorial fashion. Here are some general rules for the use of capitals; for more detailed guidelines, consult a style handbook.

- Capitalize all proper nouns and adjectives (*Vancouver Island, English, Julie, September, Shakespearean, Monday morning blues, Islamic architecture*). If you are unsure about whether to capitalize a noun or adjective, look it up in a dictionary.

- Capitalize titles that precede names (*Dr. Wong, Professor Miller*).

- Capitalize titles and offices only if a name follows (*Premier Gordon Campbell, Minister of Health Leona Aglukkaq*). If the title follows the person's name, it should not be capitalized (*Gordon Campbell became premier in 2001; Leona Aglukkaq is the first health minister from Nunavut*).

- Do not capitalize units of money (*euro, dollar, lira*), but capitalize proper adjectives that precede these units (*American dollar, British pound*). The three letter codes that are sometimes used to indicate currencies (*CAD* for Canadian dollar) are capitalized.

## Italics

Italics have now replaced underlining in all style guides. Italics should be used for emphasis (sparingly), for the titles of some works, for some foreign terms, for Latin or scientific terms, for lowercase letters in mathematical equations, for *sic* in quotations, and for words used as words.

Titles that should be italicized are usually entire works and include

- titles of books
- titles of long poems, such as ballads
- title of reports
- titles of legal cases
- titles of newspapers and magazines
- titles of movies, operas, plays, and works of art

Titles that are set in quotation marks are usually parts of a work and include

- titles of short literary works (poems, short stories)
- titles of magazine and journal articles
- titles of essays
- titles of chapters and subsections in books/works

Latin names of plants and animals are italicized. The genus is capitalized and the species/subspecies is lowercase. The first time a Latin name is used, the entire name should be used. Thereafter, the genus may be abbreviated to the first letter.

> The arbutus found in British Columbia is known by the scientific name *Arbutus menziesii*. *A. menziesii* usually grows only within eight kilometres of the ocean and is found only on the southern coast of the province.

Foreign words and phrases that have been adopted by the English language (hors d'oeuvre, virtuoso, aficionado) are not italicized. Words that have not been naturalized should be italicized. Check in a dictionary if you are unsure.

> The *Bildungsroman* originated in Germany in the eighteenth century.

> Shakespeare's tête-à-tête with Marlow did not go as he had planned.

When words are used as words within a text, they are either italicized or enclosed in quotations marks.

> Shakespeare's invention of words such as *stuff* and *belongings* exemplifies his obsession with material goods.

> A *neutron* is a subatomic particle.

> Coleridge's diction—*measureless, ceaseless*—creates a sense of infinite space.

> Her use of "crisis" to describe the situation seemed unnecessary.

# Common Confusables

There are some words that even the best writer of English will misuse from time to time. The following list contains some of the words that are most often confused and misused, with examples of how they should be used.

Accept/Except

Dylan **accepted** all the terms of his punishment **except** the no-TV rule.

*accept* = to say yes to something; *except* = everything but

Access/Excess

Linda has **access** to the account even though her debt is in **excess** of $10,000.

*access* = permission to use or enter; *excess* = more than

Adapt/Adopt

The government plans to **adopt** policies that will better **adapt** to needs in the healthcare system.

*adapt* = change to fit; *adopt* = take as one's own

Adolescents/Adolescence

Shukumar knew that **adolescence** was a difficult time for **adolescents**.

*adolescence* = the stage of life before adulthood; *adolescents* = teenagers

Adverse/Averse

Renee was **averse** to accepting the **adverse** side-effects of the botox injections.

*averse* = unwilling, opposed; *adverse* = unpleasant or negative

Advice/Advise

The counsellor **advised** him to ask his instructor for **advice** about a suitable topic.

*advise* = to offer guidance, suggest a plan of action; *advice* = counsel, guidance, recommended plan of action

Affect/Effect

The **effect** of the espresso was immediate: the caffeine **affected** her speech.

*effect* = result; *affect* = to change something or cause something to happen

Afflict/Inflict

After Brian **inflicted** the wound on the intruder, he was **afflicted** with a deep guilt.

*inflict* = to impose something bad upon someone; *afflict* = to cause distress or pain

Aggravate/Irritate

Fatima was **irritated** by her classmate's excessive use of perfume; the perfume was **aggravating** Fatima's allergies.

*irritate* = to annoy; *aggravate* = to make an existing condition worse

| All ready/Already | Moira was beside herself: her husband had **already** packed the trunk and the kids were **all ready** to go. |
|---|---|
| | *already* = something that has happened; *all ready* = each one is ready; completely ready |
| All right/Alright | When Svetlana's father asked how the exam was, she answered, "**alright**," even though she had got the questions **all right**. |
| | *all right* = each one is correct; *alright* = okay (*alright* is a colloquialism and not usually acceptable in formal writing) |
| Allusion/Illusion | The wooden boat in Mitch's daydream was not just an **illusion**—it was an **allusion** to Noah's Ark. |
| | *illusion* = something not real; *allusion* = indirect reference, often to a literary work |
| A lot/Allot/Alot | She **allotted a lot** of time for the students to write the exam. |
| | *a lot* = a great deal of; *allot* = to divide or distribute. Note that *alot* is not a word) |
| All together/Altogether | **All together,** now," Mrs. Dreyer said enthusiastically to her choir, even though their singing was **altogether** abysmal. |
| | *all together* = every part of a group at the same time; *altogether* = entirely |
| Allude/Elude/Illude | Even though Monica's father **alluded** to the events of the afternoon, the meaning of his lecture **eluded** Monica. She felt that her father was **illuding** her. |
| | *allude* = to make an indirect reference to; *elude* = to escape or slip away; *illude* = to deceive or trick |
| Alternate/Alternative | Mishka washed his darks and whites on **alternate** days until his landlady offered him an **alternative**: two loads per day. |
| | *alternate* = every other one; *alternative* = different (adj.) or a different method or way (noun) |
| Among/Between | Roberto shared his Snickers bar **among** his three friends. "**Between** you and me," he later told his mother, "those kids are total mooches." |
| | *among* = divided within a group of three or more; *between* = divided within a group of two |
| Amoral/Immoral | It was **immoral** of Derek to take advantage of the dog's **amorality** by stealing its toy. |
| | *amoral* = unaware of or indifferent to morals; *immoral* = actively transgressing good moral behaviour |

| | |
|---|---|
| Amount/Number | Leigh couldn't believe the **amount** of rain that Victoria received. She cringed at the **number** of umbrellas she had gone through. |
| | *amount* = sum or quantity of an uncountable noun; *number* = sum or quantity of a countable noun |
| And/Or | Guests of the party were asked to bring a drink **and/or** an appetizer. |
| | *and/or* = one or the other or both. If you mean *either*, use *or*. If you mean *both*, use *and*. |
| Anxious/Eager | Harvey was **eager** to start grade one, but his twin sister Hazel was **anxious** about being separated from her mother. |
| | *eager* = excited, keen; *anxious* = worried about |
| Any one/Anyone | **Anyone** who wants to may take **any one** of the desserts on the table. |
| | *any one* = one of a group of things or people; *anyone* = pronoun meaning *whoever* |
| Anyway/Any way/Anyways | I'll help you in **any way** I can, even though the club will be too dark to see your makeup, **anyway**. |
| | anyway = *in any case, or despite efforts;* any way = *any method possible;* anyways is a colloquial version of *anyway* and should be avoided in formal writing |
| Assure/Ensure/Insure | The dentist **assured** me that I would only feel a tiny prick. I carried a stress ball in my pocket to **ensure** that I would not break the dentist's hand instead. Bones are expensive to **insure**. |
| | *assure* = to promise, pledge, reassure; *ensure* = to make certain; *insure* = protect financially |
| Around/About | The dog running **around** the fire hydrant seemed to be **about** six months old. |
| | *around* = spatially encircling something; *about* = approximately |
| Awhile/A while | She waited **awhile** before chopping the vegetables, as the chicken would still be simmering for **a while**. |
| | *awhile* = for a time; *a while* = a period of time (preceded by *for* or *in*) |
| Backward/Backwards | The figure skater tripped and fell while trying to skate **backward**. She gave a **backward** glance to the judges before realizing with horror that her uniform was on **backwards**. |
| | *backward* is used when acting as an adjective (*backward* glance); directionally, *backward* is preferred; *backwards* is acceptable as an adverb meaning *the wrong way*. |

| | |
|---|---|
| Bad/Badly | I feel **bad** because I did **badly** on my test. I hate getting **bad** marks.<br><br>*bad* = adjective or subject of a linking verb; *badly* = adverb |
| Beside/Besides | "**Besides**," Sibel said to her mother, "your note wasn't even **beside** the cookies."<br><br>*Besides* = in addition to something (figuratively); *beside* = next to (physically) |
| Born/Borne | Ever since Arun was **born**, he has **borne** many hardships.<br><br>*born* = came into life; *borne* = past tense of *bear*; to endure |
| Bring/Take | **Bring** your cookie cutters when you come over here, and then **take** the cookies back home with you.<br><br>*bring* = to carry toward, come with; *take* = to carry away from, go with |
| Can/May | **May** I borrow your shampoo? I **can** always count on you to have quality styling products.<br><br>*may* = to have permission; *can* = to be able to |
| Capital/Capitol | The teacher corrected Dominic's work by putting a **capital** letter on the **capital** city of Washington, D.C. It was there, she wrote in the margin, that the **Capitol** Building was located.<br><br>*capital* = used for cities and letters; *capitol* = a type of building, usually an American state legislature building |
| Censor/Censure/Sensor | The publisher was **censured** for having **censored** the contents of the young author's novel, in which a juvenile delinquent disables the motion **sensor** on a company security device.<br><br>*censor* = to delete questionable or offensive material; *censure* = to publicly criticize; *sensor* = an electronic or mechanical detector |
| Collaborate/Corroborate | Mr. Peterson and Mr. Naylor **collaborated** on the survey; its findings **corroborated** their theory.<br><br>*collaborate = to work together; corroborate = to support or validate* |
| Common/Mutual | Because Marika and Juliana had so many **common** insecurities, they were constantly plagued by a need for **mutual** reassurance.<br><br>*common* = shared; *mutual* = reciprocal |
| Compare to/Compare with | Jaya **compared** the blind date **to** her last trip to the dentist. The two were equally painful. *She compared the meal with* |

*the one she had made at home the week before, and found that the two were comparable in taste.*

*compare to* = find similarities between unlike things; *compare with* = find similarities between like things

Complement/Compliment    Samuel **complimented** Mona on her vase, which he felt **complemented** her antique table perfectly.

*complement* = to complete or raise to perfection or match; *compliment* = to praise or flatter

Comprise/Compose/Constitute/Consist of    Claude's dinner **consisted** of a pizza, a milkshake, and a box of donuts, typical of the meals he **composed** for himself. The milkshake **comprised** bananas and ice cream. All this **constituted** half of Claude's daily caloric intake.

*comprise* = to include, contain; *compose* = to make up; *constitute* = to form, compose; *consist of* = to be made up of

Conscience/Conscious    Emmet was **conscious** of the fact that everyone in the class hated the substitute teacher; however, his **conscience** wouldn't let him join in the spitball-firing.

*conscience* = moral centre; *conscious* = aware; awake

Consequent(ly)/Subsequent(ly)    Souad ate all the Reese's Pieces in the package; **consequently**, she felt ill. **Subsequently**, she decided to buy some double-stuffed Oreos.

*consequently* = as a result; *subsequently* = coming after (not necessarily caused by previous events)

Content/Contents    So far, the **content** of the film was tame. All that had happened was that a lady tripped and spilled the **contents** of her purse.

*content* = subject, topic of a book, film, etc.; *contents* = the things contained in something

Continual/Continuous    The next door neighbour's dog **continually** barked. One evening, Philip played his stereo **continuously** to drown out the sound.

*continual* = frequently repeated; *continuous* = nonstop or uninterrupted

Council/Counsel    The **council** of directors gave the **client** legal counsel.

*council* = a group or assembly that consults or advises; *counsel* = advice or recommendations

Criteria/Criterion    Guy shuddered when he looked at the **criteria** his lab report had to meet. As he read each **criterion**, he saw how much work he had left to do.

*criterion* = a standard for judgment; *criteria* is the plural of *criterion*.

| | |
|---|---|
| Defuse/Diffuse | As the ceiling fan **diffused** the cigarette smoke throughout the room, Ian knew that once again he would have to **defuse** a stressful situation. |
| | *diffuse* = to spread; *defuse* = to make less tense or dangerous |
| Discreet/Discrete | Dawn was **discreet** in the application of her new perfume, which came in a kit with five **discrete** parts. |
| | *discreet* = subtle or judicious; *discrete* = distinct or separate |
| Discriminating/Discriminatory | Dorian was **discriminating** in his choice of clothing stores, many of which he found **discriminatory** against men. |
| | *discriminating* = careful, analytical; *discriminatory* = biased |
| Disinterested/Uninterested | Antoine wished he were a **disinterested** party at this function, so he could slip out. He yawned, completely **uninterested** in the speech the vice-president was giving. |
| | *disinterested* = impartial, without a stake; *uninterested* = bored, without interest |
| Dual/Duel | The **dual** nature of Wesley's personality often led his saloon-mates to challenge him to **duels**. |
| | *dual* = double; *duel* = a prearranged fight with weapons |
| Economic/Economical | Alejandro's father was an expert on **economic** policy, but he was anything but **economical** in his spending habits. |
| | *economic* = pertaining to the economy; *economical* = thrifty |
| Elicit/Illicit | The psychiatrist could not **elicit** a response when she questioned her client about his **illicit** relationship with his company's Purolator courier. |
| | *elicit* = to draw out; *illicit* = not permitted for legal or moral reasons |
| Eminent/Imminent/Immanent | The **eminent** bachelor stood on the deck of his yacht, waiting for the **imminent** storm. He sighed and said, "disappointment is **immanent** in human nature." |
| | *eminent* = distinguished, noteworthy; *imminent* = about to occur; *immanent* = dwelling within something |
| Envelop/envelope | The mysterious woman feared the smoke would **envelop** her as she dropped the cream-coloured **envelope** into the mail slot. |
| | *envelop* = to enshroud or surround; *envelope* = holder for a letter |
| Every day/Everyday | Thanh's girlfriend sent him love letters **every day** she was away; for most people, such attention was not an **everyday** occurrence. |
| | *every day* = each day; *everyday* = normal, usual |

| | |
|---|---|
| Every one/Everyone | **Every one** of the jury members sitting around the table knew that nobody was going anywhere unless **everyone** agreed on the verdict. |
| | *every one* = each part of a group; *everyone* = everybody |
| Evoke/Invoke | Hardeep tried to **invoke** the spirit of Edgar Allen Poe in her poetry reading; her words **evoked** images of crows, cobwebs, and windy cliffsides. |
| | *invoke* = to actively call forth or appeal to something; *evoke* = to call up, summon |
| Explicit/Implicit | Jordan's desire to date his classmate was **explicit** in the note he passed her in third period algebra. The teacher's concerns for Jordan's priorities were **implicit** in the comments she wrote on his report card. |
| | *explicit* = deliberately spelled out; *implicit* = not stated outright but implied |
| Famous/Notable/Notorious | The **famous** museum featured the **notable** Thomas Edison and the **notorious** Jack the Ripper. |
| | *famous* = renowned, well-known; *notable* = praiseworthy; *notorious* = having a bad reputation |
| Farther/Further | "I don't like adventure sports. You couldn't be any **further** from the truth," Marcia said with a pout, as Rock drove his Jeep **farther** down the sand dune. |
| | *farther* = at a greater physical distance; *further* = at a greater figurative distance |
| Flaunt/Flout | Inge **flouted** the kitchen's no-jewelry rule as she **flaunted** her new diamond bracelet in front of the minimum-wage dish-washer. |
| | *flout* = to purposely disregard or disdain; *flaunt* = to show off |
| Fewer/Less | Harvey had **fewer** household responsibilities than his wife, but he also had **less** time at home. |
| | *fewer* = of a smaller number (used for countable things); *less* = of a smaller amount (used for non-countable things) |
| Flair/Flare | Sierra had a **flair** for disruptive behaviour, including setting off **flares** in the hallway of her high school. This usually occurred when her anxiety issues **flared** up. |
| | *flair* = knack, talent; *flare* = a device that produces bright light (noun); to become aggravated (verb) |
| Good/Well | Katie did really **well** on her sociology exam. She was having a **good** day. |
| | *good* = adjective; *well* = adverb |

| | |
|---|---|
| Had/Had of | If I **had** checked the laundry room before I left, I would **have** seen water gushing from the washing machine. |
| | *Had of* is incorrect; *had* is the correct usage. |
| Hanged/Hung | Right before Rodney **hanged** himself, he **hung** his latest painting on the wall above the toilet. |
| | *hanged* = killed by hanging; *hung* = suspended (used to describe objects) |
| Historic/Historical | February 22, 2010 will become a **historic** day for Canadian ice dancers. The drama director opted for her students to dress in **historical** war costumes. |
| | *historic* = important, momentous; *historical* = relating to the past |
| If/Whether | Let me know **whether** you want condiments on your hot dog. Tell me **if** you want a sundae afterwards. |
| | *whether* = implies alternatives; *if* = implies uncertainty, can be used for future conditions |
| Immigrate/Emigrate | The Chiang family **emigrated** from Taiwan in 1997. The Chiang family **immigrated** to Canada in 1997. |
| | *emigrate* = to leave one country (use with *from*); *immigrate* = to arrive in another (use with *to*) |
| Imply/Infer | Sawyer **inferred** from the principal's manner that the students were to quiet down; the principal had **implied** as much with his stern glances in Sawyer's direction. |
| | *imply* = to hint or suggest (done by the speaker, writer); *infer* = to deduce (done by the listener, reader) |
| In/In to/Into | Paul lounged **in** the swimming pool. When the phone rang, he went **in to** answer it. He forgot he had closed the sliding door and walked **into** it, smashing his nose on the glass. |
| | *in* = preposition; *in to* = used when *to* is part of the verb ; *into* = implies movement toward |
| In regards/In regard | **In regard** to the skateboarding proposal, the council president gave a definite "no." |
| | *In regards to* is incorrect. Use *in regard to* or *with regard to* instead. *Regards* is a term used at the end of a letter in place of *yours* or *sincerely*. |
| Ingenious/Ingenuous | Mary Sue stared up at Billy with a sweet and **ingenuous** expression. She thought his newest creation, a self-emptying garbage can, was **ingenious**. |
| | *ingenious* = smart, clever; *ingenuous* = candid, naïve |
| Instants/Instance | The worst **instance** of poor driving I ever saw was when, after several **instants** of fishtailing, a lady drove her SUV through a |

barrier and into a snowbank. There are many other **instances** of bad driving that I could tell you about.

*instants* = plural of *instant*, meaning moments; *instance* = a case or example of something; *instances* = plural of *instance*

Irregardless/Regardless    Katherine decided to enjoy herself **regardless** of whether her husband would be there.

*regardless* = without concern for, indifferent; *irregardless* is not a word

Its/It's    Jessica looked at the dog and said, "**It's** licking **its** paw again."

*its* = possessive; *it's* = contraction of *it is*

Kind of/Sort of    A beagle is a **kind of** dog. A trowel is a **sort of** shovel.

Do not use *kind of* or *sort of* to mean *somewhat*.

Lead/Led    As they approached the street, Mrs. Headley **led** her daughter across by the hand. Her son Harry yelled to his sister, "get the **lead** out of your feet!"

*lead* = a heavy metal; *led* = past tense of the verb *lead*

Lie/Lay/Laid    Dr. Perry told his patient to **lie** on the examining table and **lay** her belongings down on one of the chairs. She **laid** her jacket on the chair by the door and **lay** down on the table.

*lie* = to recline or rest in a horizontal position; *lay* = past tense of *lie*; *lay* = to put or place (something); *laid* = past tense of *lay*

Like/As/Such as    I was bitten by a mosquito or something **like** it. **As** I was standing on my inflatable bed waving a shoe around, I lost my balance. My plan did not go **as** I hoped. My friend offered suggestions for my predicament, **such as** moving to another tent and leaving her in peace.

*like* suggests resemblance and is used between two nouns (he is *like* a cat); *as* suggests resemblance and is used between a noun and an adjective (he is *as* red *as* a strawberry); *as* = while; *such as* = including, for example

Literally/Figuratively    Her nasty dog **literally** bites the hand that feeds him.

*Literally* = actually; do not use *literally* when you mean *figuratively*, such as in the sentence "I *literally* laughed my head off." (Your head did not fall off.)

Loan/Loaned/Lend    When Jocelyn got fired, her friend offered to **lend** her his PlayStation to cheer her up. Jocelyn said she would prefer a **loan** of a thousand dollars. Grudgingly, he **loaned** her the money, and **lent** her the PlayStation anyway, "just in case."

*loan* = used with money; *loaned* = past tense of *loan*; *lend* = used with other items; *lent* = past tense of *lend*)

| | |
|---|---|
| Loose/Lose | My drawstrings are so **loose** that I may **lose** these pants before the evening is over. |
| | *loose* = not tight; *lose* = to misplace, to fail to win |
| Manner/Manor | Felix didn't like the **manner** in which the butler was walking out of the **manor**. |
| | *manner* = way; *manor* = a house on an estate |
| Maybe/May be | Okay, **maybe** I'll go. But I really think the party at Kady's place **may be** better. |
| | *maybe* = (adverb) perhaps; *may be* = (verb) could be |
| Moral/Morale | The coach never went against his **morals**, so he told his team about their uniforms getting lost even though it risked lowering the team's **morale**. |
| | *moral* = principle, teaching; *morale* = spirit |
| Of/Off of | During its nap, the cat rolled **off** the table. |
| | *The extra* of *in* off of *is not needed;* off *is correct.* |
| On/On to/Onto/Upon | Jo's favourite reality show was **on** at nine o'clock. She put the kettle **on to** make tea. When she got back to the living room, her dog Velcro had jumped **onto** the couch. She knew he would only get off her case **upon** being fed. |
| | *on* = preposition; *on to* = used when *to* is part of the verb that follows; *onto* = implies motion; *upon* = introduces a condition |
| Oral/Aural/Verbal | The **oral** surgeon had a **verbal** contract with the dental hygienists regarding the practice of listening to Josh Groban at work. He believed that such **aural** distractions would negatively affect their work. |
| | *oral* = of the mouth; *aural* = of the ear; *verbal* = of words |
| Passed/Past | Joseph **passed** judgment on his fiancée's **past** indiscretions. |
| | *passed* = past tense of verb *to pass*; *past* = previous |
| Perspective/Prospective | Miguel had a fresh **perspective** after interviewing **prospective** renters. |
| | *perspective* = viewpoint; *prospective* = possible |
| Populous/Populace | The new town was more **populous** but more boring than the one they had come from. The entire **populace** seemed to plan their weekends around Saturday night bingo. |
| | *populous* = heavily populated; *populace* = inhabitants of a place |
| Pore/Pour | Valerie **poured** herself another cup of coffee and **pored** over her biology notes for the next day's exam. |
| | *pore* (over) = to read intently; *pour* = to cause a liquid to flow |

| | |
|---|---|
| Practical/Practicable | Although a self-emptying dishwasher would be very **practical**, it is not a **practicable** solution to laziness.<br>*practical* = useful, sensible; *practicable* = feasible |
| Precede/Proceed | Before you **proceed** across the street, look left and right. Remember that accidents are always **preceded** by carelessness.<br>*precede* = to come before; *proceed* = to go forward |
| Principal/Principle | The **principal** reason that all the students hated the **principal** was that he started every morning announcement over the PA with a daily grammar **principle**.<br>*principal* = head of school (noun), main (adj); *principle* = a rule |
| Purposely/Purposefully | Jared **purposely** threw his binder into the mud puddle and **purposefully** strode toward the school's parking lot. He had had enough.<br>*purposely* = on purpose, intentionally; *purposefully* = determinedly, with a goal in mind |
| Quote/Quotation | Paris overheard that her teacher liked **quotations** in essays, so she **quoted** every author she read.<br>*quote* is the verb; *quotation* is the noun |
| Raise/Rise | Melissa was taught two rules as a child: **rise** early and **raise** your hand before speaking.<br>*raise* = to lift or bring something up (requires an object); *rise* = to get up (does not take an object) |
| Real/Really | Nektaria said that it was **really** easy to bake muffins. Her mother smiled and thought, "wait until you have to use a **real** oven."<br>*real* (adj)= true, proper; *really* (adv) = very; do not use *real* to mean *really* |
| Refrain/Restrain | Please **refrain** from jumping out the window while the train is in motion. Anyone caught attempting to break this rule will be **restrained** until the train arrives at the next station.<br>*refrain (from)* = stop (yourself); *restrain* = physically hold back |
| Regretfully/Regrettably | **Regretfully**, the camp counselor turned to the campers and told them, "**Regrettably**, we can't go on our canoe trip in this storm."<br>*regretfully* = with regret (used with people); *regrettably* = unfortunately |
| Replace/Substitute | I **replaced** my old Honda with a new BMW. I **substituted** a new BMW for my old Honda.<br>*replace with* = use when the object of the verb is the old item; *substituted for* = use when the object of the verb is the new item |

| | |
|---|---|
| Respectful/Respective | Eva was very **respectful** as she presented the math and science awards to the **respective** recipients. |
| | *respectful* = polite; *respective* = separate |
| Revolve/Rotate | As the figure skater **rotated** on one skate, she thought, "my life **revolves** around this sport." |
| | *revolve* = to move around something else; *rotate* = to turn around in one place |
| Sensual/Sensuous | While watching the **sensual** love scene in the film, Rami had the **sensuous** experience of eating a mandarin orange. |
| | *Sensual* has a sexual connotation; *sensuous* = involving the senses |
| Sight/Site/Cite | Beau did a double take at the **sight** of the men at the construction **site** standing around and talking. He made a note to later **cite** a quotation about laziness in his progress report. |
| | *sight* = something you see; *site* = a place; *cite* = to make reference to (a quotation) |
| Some time/Sometime/Sometimes | **Some time** ago, I decided that I would visit Disneyland **sometime**. **Sometimes** when my friends talk about the giant Disney characters, I wish that I had got around to going. |
| | *some time* = a while; *sometime* = at an unspecified time in the future; *sometimes* = occasionally |
| Stationary/Stationery | While riding on her **stationary** bike, Bridget made a mental note that she needed to buy **stationery** for work. |
| | *stationary* = not moving; *stationery* = office supplies |
| Supposed to/Suppose | Arya forgot that he was **supposed to** buy milk on his way home from school. He **supposed** he could buy some after work. |
| | *supposed to* = meant to; *suppose to* is incorrect; *suppose* = to think |
| Than/Then | Marie ate the jelly donut. **Then** she discovered that it was even better **than** the chocolate one. |
| | *than* = used in comparisons; *then* = at that time |
| That/Which/Who | The computer **that** I ordered arrived severely damaged; its screen, **which** wasn't as big as I remembered, looked as if a cat had scratched it. The man **who** had sold me the computer was obviously a shady character. |
| | *That* should be used for restrictive clauses (when no comma is used); *which* should be used for non-restrictive clauses (after a comma); *who* should be used for human beings. |

| | |
|---|---|
| Their/There/They're | **They're** not going to be **there** for **their** graduation.<br><br>*they're* = contraction of *they are*; *there* = in or at a specified place; *their* = possessive form of *they* |
| To/Two/Too | Aiden took his **two** sisters **to** Baskin Robbins after supper because he wanted to buy them dessert, **too**.<br><br>*to* = preposition or part of an infinitive; *two* = *number*; *too* = *also* |
| Torturous/Tortuous | Valentina ran down the **tortuous** path in the woods, trying to forget the **torturous** details of the film she had just watched.<br><br>*torturous* = having to do with torture; *tortuous* = twisting and turning |
| Use/Utilize | Choon **utilized** the whisk to make his omelette, but it was a lost cause. He should have **used** his phone instead to order a cake.<br><br>*Use* and *utilize* both mean *make use of*. Choose *use* over *utilize* to avoid sounding overly formal or technical. |
| Used to/Use to | Andrei remembered the days when he **used to** enjoy school. Which car can I **use** to drive to university?<br><br>*Used to* is the correct form to illustrate past behaviour |
| Wait on/Wait for | As Kendra **waited on** table seven, she anxiously **waited for** ten o'clock, when her shift would end.<br><br>*wait on* = serve; *wait for* = anticipate events |
| Whether (or not) | Dmitri decided he would buy avocados **whether or not** they were on sale. He didn't know **whether** he had enough money for strawberries.<br><br>*whether* = if; *whether or not* = no matter if (used for two possible conditions) |
| Who's/Whose | **Who's** coming to the party tonight? **Whose** is it again?<br><br>*who's* = *contraction of who is*; *whose* = *possessive pronoun* |
| You're/Your | **You're** stepping on **your** shoelaces again.<br><br>*You're* = *contraction of you are*; *your* = *possessive pronoun* |

# Word Roots, Prefixes, and Affixes

## COMMON WORD ROOTS

| Root | Meaning | Examples |
|---|---|---|
| *bene* | good, well | *beneficial, benediction* |
| *bio* | living, of life | *biodiversity, biochemistry* |
| *duc(e)* | lead or make | *ductile, deduce, produce* |
| *gen* | production of, of race, of descent | *generate, gene, gender* |
| *geo* | of earth | *geology, geography* |
| *graph* | written | *cartography, graphomania* |
| *jur, jus, jud* | of law | *justice, judicial, jury* |
| *log(o)* | of words, speech | *logograph, logotype* |
| *luc* | of light | *translucent, lucid* |
| *manu* | of hand | *manuscript, manufacture* |
| *mit, mis* | of sending | *transmit, missal* |
| *path* | of feeling, suffering | *pathology, sympathetic* |
| *phil(e)* | of love | *bibliophile, philanthropic* |
| *photo* | of light | *photosynthesis* |
| *port* | of carrying | *transportation, portable* |
| *psyche* | soul | *psychology* |
| *scrib, scrip* | of writing | *scribble, scribner, transcript* |
| *sent* | of feeling | *resent, sentiment* |

## COMMON PREFIXES

### Negative and Positive Prefixes

| Prefix | Meaning | Examples |
|---|---|---|
| *a* | without | *apathetic, amoral* |
| *anti* | against | *antimony, antibody* |
| *contra, counter, con* | against, opposing | *contradictory, counterproductive, contest* |
| *de* | remove | *debase, depose* |
| *dis* | apart, away | *disparate, disapprove* |
| *il, im, in, ir* | not | *illogical, illegitimate, impatient, inept, irrational* |

| Prefix | Meaning | Examples |
|--------|---------|----------|
| mal | bad, wrong | malevolent, malcontent, malfunction |
| mis | wrong | mistaken, misspelling |
| non | not | nonaggressive |
| pro | on the side of | protest, proaction |
| pseudo | false, imitating | pseudonym |
| un | not | untidy, unappreciated |

## Number Prefixes

| Prefix | Meaning | Examples |
|--------|---------|----------|
| uni, mono | one | uniform, monochrome |
| bi, di | two | bicycle, carbon dioxide |
| tri | three | triathlon, tricycle |
| quad, tetra | four | tetrameter, quadruped |
| demi | lesser, half | demigod, demitasse |
| sem(i) | half | semester, semicolon |

## Space Prefixes

| Prefix | Meaning | Examples |
|--------|---------|----------|
| arch | highest | archbishop, archenemy |
| circum | around, about | circumvent, circumscribe |
| e(x) | former, out of, from | ex-husband, exile, excrete |
| inter | between, among | intermingle, intermarry |
| mega | large | megaphone |
| micro | small | microfilm, microcosm |
| out | to the greatest extent | outlast, outperform |
| pre, pro | before | preconceive, proclaim |
| re | back again | return, rerun, reread |
| sub | under, inferior | submarine, sublet |
| super, sur | above, beyond, over | superlative, superscript, surname, survive |
| syn | with, together | synonym, synthesis |
| trans | across | translate, transatlantic |

## COMMON SUFFIXES

| Prefix | Meaning | Examples |
|---|---|---|
| *able, ible* | capable of being | *understandable, drinkable, edible* |
| *dom* | rank, state | *freedom, kingdom* |
| *eer, er, or* | one who | *instructor, painter, volunteer* |
| *ery* | condition | *slavery* |
| *ese, ish, (i)an* | nationality, pertaining to | *Chinese, Australian, Flemish, Freudian* |
| *ess* | female | *actress, laundress* |
| *ette* | imitation, small, compact | *flanellette, kitchenette* |
| *ism* | doctrine, theory | *Darwinism, communism* |
| *ite, ist* | member of, part of | *socialite, Jesuite, communist* |
| *ity* | the quality of | *equality* |
| *ize* | cause to become | *cauterize, magnetize* |
| *less* | without | *worthless, careless* |
| *let* | small, insignificant | *piglet, booklet* |
| *ment* | condition, state of | *excitement, refreshment* |
| *ness* | the state of | *blindness* |
| *ship* | condition, state of | *leadership, friendship* |
| *ster* | worker, agent | *gangster, trickster* |

**Notes**

# Index

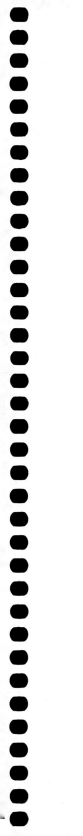